OH, CANADA! THE MAPLE LEAF'S JOURNEY TO STARS AND STRIPES

Oh, Canada! The Maple Leaf's Journey to Stars and Stripes

JD ROSSETTI

CONTENTS

FORWORD

What If Canada Became a U.S. State?

"Welcome to the United States of Eh?"

What if one day you woke up, turned on the news, and saw the headline: "Canada Votes to Join the U.S.!" Would you be shocked? Would you celebrate? Would you panic about the fate of poutine and free healthcare?

Welcome to the wildest geopolitical "What If?" of the century!

In Oh, Canada: The Maple Leaf's Journey to Stars and Stripes, we take you on a rollercoaster ride of diplomacy, politics, and culture, exploring what would happen if Canada—the friendly neighbor with better manners and stronger beer—decided to merge with the United States of America.

From constitutional chaos to cultural clashes, political upheaval to economic transformation, this book breaks down every hilarious, bizarre, and surprisingly serious angle of Canada becoming the 51st state... or maybe the 51st through 60th states (because let's face it, Quebec probably won't go quietly).

Why You NEED to Read This Book

A Hilarious Yet Insightful Political Analysis
- What would happen to Canada's beloved universal healthcare if it had to compete with America's health insurance horror show?

- Would Tim Hortons become the official coffee of Congress, or would Starbucks strike first?

- Would Canadians finally stop apologizing so much, or would U.S. politicians start saying "sorry" more? (Okay, probably not.)

A Deep Dive into the Pros, Cons, and Absolute Madness of a Canada-USA Merger

- Could this actually happen legally, or is it just a political fever dream?

- Would the NHL become the official religion of the new state(s)?

- Would Quebec demand independence immediately, or would they just laugh in French and watch the whole thing burn?

A Serious Political and Economic Thought Experiment (Disguised as a Fun Read!)

- How would the U.S. Electoral College change? Would this permanently alter American politics?

- What happens to Canada's military, natural resources, and international reputation?

- Would Canadians lose their politeness, superior gun control, and superior bacon in the process?

What the Experts (and Probably Your Neighbor) Are Saying

"This book is like reading a political thriller, a history lesson, and a stand-up comedy routine all in one!" – Some Random Political Science Professor

"If you've ever wondered what would happen if Canada and the U.S. fused like some kind of North American Voltron, this book is your answer." – A Guy Who Loves Both Countries

"I came for the political analysis, stayed for the dad jokes, and now I'm terrified for the future of Canadian poutine." – A Concerned Canadian

A Chapter Sneak Peek!

- Chapter 6: The Pros of Canada Joining the U.S. – More military power, bigger economy, and universal access to Olive Garden!
- Chapter 9: Healthcare Showdown: Universal Care vs. 'Please Sell Your Kidney to Pay This Bill' – Would Canadians survive the transition?
- Chapter 15: Would Canada Even Want This? – Spoiler alert: Probably not, but let's have fun imagining the chaos!
- Chapter 22: International Reactions – Would the rest of the world be shocked, thrilled, or start placing bets on which country joins next?
- Chapter 29: Future Predictions – In 50 years, would Canada be flourishing as the northern superstate... or trying to secede?

Final Thought: Is This Pure Fiction or a Future Reality?

Some might call this a fun thought experiment, others might see it as an eerie glimpse into a potential future. Either way, Oh, Canada: The Maple Leaf's Journey to Stars and Stripes is a must-read for anyone who loves politics, history, economics, or just a good dose of international absurdity.

So grab your hockey stick, maple syrup, and a copy of this book—because if Canada ever does become part of the U.S., you'll want to be the one at the dinner table saying, "I totally saw this coming!"

DISCLAIMER: No Canadian geese were harmed in the making of this book.

| 1 |

Introduction: The Geopolitical Landscape of Canada

An engaging introduction to Canada's current geopolitical status, setting the stage for the exploration of potential statehood.

Main Points and Objectives:

• Overview of Canada's Position: Discuss Canada's role in global politics, its alliances, and its standing in international organizations.

• Domestic Political Climate: Examine the current political environment within Canada, including recent elections and policy directions.

• Pros and Cons of Statehood: Introduce the foundational principles of the advantages and disadvantages of Canada becoming a U.S. state.

• Feasibility Considerations: Present an overview of the practical steps and challenges in such a transition.

Fun Fact: Did you know that Canada and the U.S. share the longest undefended border in the world, stretching over 5,500 miles?

Welcome to the Hypothetical but Highly Entertaining Thought Experiment

Canada: the land of maple syrup, hockey, and apologizing even when someone else bumps into you. But beneath this stereotype of unparalleled niceness lies a geopolitical powerhouse—a country that, despite its friendly demeanor, holds significant sway in global affairs.

Now, imagine if one day, instead of saying "Sorry," Canada said, "Stars and Stripes, here we come!" That's right—what if Canada, in a fit of constitutional curiosity (or economic opportunism), decided to join the United States as the 51st (or more like the 51st through 60th) state(s)?

In this book, we explore this delightful, perplexing, and slightly terrifying hypothetical scenario. But before we dive into the nitty-gritty of statehood, let's set the stage by understanding Canada's current geopolitical status, alliances, and domestic climate.

Buckle up, grab a double-double from Tim Hortons, and let's begin.

Overview of Canada's Position in Global Politics

While the U.S. is often seen as the loud, extroverted leader of the global stage, Canada has mastered the role of the respected, diplomatic best friend—the kind of country that brings snacks to meetings, never raises its voice, and somehow convinces everyone to get along.

Canada's Global Influence: More Than Just a U.S. Sidekick

Canada isn't just America's quieter neighbor; it's a major player in international organizations:
- NATO Member: Canada contributes to military operations but prefers peacekeeping over war-starting (think of Canada as the friend who holds your earrings during a fight but never throws a punch).

- G7 & G20 Participant: A member of the world's top economic clubs—kind of like being in an exclusive golf league, but for finance ministers.
- The United Nations: A key supporter of international peace, climate initiatives, and diplomacy.
- USMCA Agreement: A.k.a. "NAFTA 2.0," which ensures that Canada, the U.S., and Mexico remain economically tangled together like a trio in a three-legged race.

So while Canada may not boast the military muscle of the U.S. or the economic heft of China, it punches above its weight in diplomacy, trade, and global stability. But would this influence increase or decrease if Canada traded its independent identity for statehood?

Canada's Domestic Political Climate: What's Brewing in the Great White North?

At first glance, Canadian politics might look similar to the U.S.—they both have elections, debates, and occasional scandals involving inappropriate political handshakes. But under the surface, Canada's system is remarkably different.

How Canada's Government Works (And Why It's Not the U.S.)

Unlike the U.S. system of government, which is based on a presidential democracy, Canada operates under a parliamentary democracy:
- Instead of a President, Canada has a Prime Minister (PM). Think of the PM as the head coach, but instead of being elected directly, they are chosen by the party that wins the most seats in Parliament.
- Instead of a Congress, Canada has a House of Commons and a Senate, but—get this—the Senate isn't elected; it's appointed by the Prime Minister. Imagine if U.S. Senators were hand-picked by the President... Yeah, exactly.

- Canada has a multi-party system, meaning elections are not a two-party brawl like in the U.S. but more like a hockey brawl involving five to six teams.

Currently, political tensions in Canada revolve around issues like:
- Healthcare (which is free but has long wait times)
- Oil & Gas (a.k.a. "Should we keep drilling or hug more trees?")
- Climate Change (spoiler alert: it's cold, but still happening!)
- Regional divides (Quebec still side-eyeing the rest of Canada)

Would statehood smooth these issues out, or just make them America's problem?

Pros and Cons of Canada Becoming a U.S. State

Alright, let's get into the meat (or tofu, for our vegetarian friends) of the debate: Would statehood be a good or bad idea?

Pros:
* Economic Growth: Canada's GDP would be absorbed into the U.S., creating an economic powerhouse larger than China's.
* No More Currency Exchange: Canadians wouldn't have to cringe at exchange rates when shopping in the U.S. (Goodbye, expensive Florida vacations!)
* Easier Travel: No more border checks, passport stamps, or explaining to TSA why you have maple syrup in your carry-on.
* Stronger Military Power: Canada would gain access to the biggest defense budget on the planet (but would they want it?).

Cons:
* Loss of National Identity: Would Canada still be... Canada? Or just "North Montana"?
* Political Clashes: Canada leans more left politically—how would its healthcare, social policies, and gun laws mix with the U.S.?

* Quebec Would Have a Meltdown: Let's be real—if Canada joined the U.S., Quebec might just pack up and join France instead.

* Hockey Rule Changes? (shudders in Canadian)

Feasibility Considerations: How Would This Even Happen?

Even if Canadians suddenly woke up and decided "Yes, let's do this", the road to statehood would be longer than a Canadian winter.

- Step 1: National Referendum – Canada would need a nationwide vote, and honestly... good luck with that.

- Step 2: U.S. Congress Approval – The U.S. would need to rewrite a few rules to admit a country, not just a state.

- Step 3: Provincial Negotiations – Could each province join separately, or would they have to stick together like an awkward road trip?

- Step 4: Cultural Adjustment – Would Tim Hortons be legally required to compete with Dunkin' Donuts? Would the U.S. adopt "eh" into official government documents?

Fun Fact:

Did you know that Canada and the U.S. share the longest undefended border in the world, stretching over 5,500 miles? That's enough space to fit over 30 million hockey rinks! (And yes, we did the math.)

Final Thought: Should Canada and the U.S. Swipe Right on Each Other?

As we dive deeper into this book, we'll explore the history, politics, economics, and sheer ridiculousness of a U.S.-Canada merger. Could it work? Would it work? Should it work?

For now, keep an open mind—and maybe a backup supply of maple syrup. This is going to be a wild ride.

So how did Canada get its name anyway?

A group of early explorers sat around trying to come up with a name for the new land.

One of them said, "Let's put letters in a hat and draw them out one by one."

So they did, and the first letter they pulled was C, eh?

Then N, eh?

Then D, eh?

And that's how we got C-eh-N-eh-D-eh!

| 2 |

Historical Ties: From Colonies to Neighbors

C Explore the shared history of Canada and the United States, highlighting moments of cooperation and conflict.

Main Points and Objectives:
• Colonial Roots: Discuss the parallel colonial histories and the divergence leading to separate nations.
• War of 1812: Examine the conflict that pitted the two nations against each other and its lasting impact.
• Trade Relations: Trace the evolution of economic ties from the 19th century to present day.
• Cultural Exchanges: Highlight the flow of people, ideas, and culture across the border over the centuries.
Fun Fact: The term "O.K." was popularized during the War of 1812, symbolizing "Old Kinderhook," a nickname for President Martin Van Buren.

How the U.S. and Canada Went from Frenemies to BFFs (Mostly)

Once Upon a Time... There Were Two Colonies

Long before the U.S. and Canada became the world's most polite set of neighbors, they were just two scrappy little colonies under British rule—kind of like two kids in the same classroom who both had to do whatever the teacher (King George III) said.

However, while the thirteen colonies in the South were plotting how to kick the teacher out of the classroom, the northern colonies (now Canada) were more like, "Eh, let's wait this one out."

And thus, the great divergence began!

Colonial Roots: One Revolution, Two Paths

By the late 1700s, the British-controlled territories in North America were divided into two very different groups:

1. The American Colonies (a.k.a. The Rebellious Teenagers)
- Tired of taxes, tea tariffs, and British rules.
- Declared independence in 1776, creating what would eventually become the United States of America.
- Decided democracy was a DIY project and immediately started arguing over how to run their new country (spoiler: they're still arguing).

2. The Northern Colonies (a.k.a. The Loyalists Who Preferred Free Healthcare and Poutine)
- These colonies—Nova Scotia, Quebec, Ontario (then Upper and Lower Canada), and the Maritimes—stayed loyal to Britain.
- Many British loyalists from the American Revolution fled north to Canada, giving the region a boost in British influence and a sudden influx of people who hated Thomas Jefferson.
- Instead of joining the revolution, Canada opted for a slower, more polite break from Britain that involved fewer muskets and more patient negotiations.

Thus, from the very beginning, the U.S. and Canada were like siblings who chose wildly different life paths—one went the "angsty teenager who moves out at 18" route, and the other stayed home until it was financially stable enough to move out at 100 (Canada officially gained independence in 1867 but still kept ties to the British monarchy—talk about a long break-up).

The War of 1812: The Time the U.S. Tried (and Failed) to Conquer Canada

Now, if there's one moment in history where Canada and the U.S. almost became one nation—but didn't—it's the War of 1812.

So What Was the War of 1812, and Why Should You Care?
- It was basically Round 2 of the American Revolution, except this time, the U.S. fought against both Britain AND Canada.
- The U.S. was mad about British naval blockades and trade restrictions, but they also thought, "Hey, while we're at it, let's invade Canada!"
- President James Madison assumed that Canada would be easy to take over, believing Canadians would welcome U.S. troops as liberators (Spoiler alert: They did not).

How Did That Work Out?
- U.S. forces tried invading Canada multiple times. None of them worked.
- The British and Canadian militias (including Indigenous allies) burned down Washington, D.C. in 1814, just to make a point.
- Fun fact: This was the only time in U.S. history that the White House was set on fire by a foreign army.
- The war ended in a stalemate, but Canadians walked away feeling extra smug about having successfully defended their land.

- The U.S. never attempted to invade Canada again (unless you count college students on spring break).

Trade Relations: From Tariffs to Besties

After the whole "we tried to conquer you" thing didn't work out, the U.S. and Canada gradually warmed up to each other—mostly because of money.

Throughout the 19th and 20th centuries, trade between the two countries grew, leading to major economic agreements like:

- The Reciprocity Treaty (1854): An early attempt at a free trade deal (which the U.S. later canceled—because Congress has commitment issues).
- The Auto Pact (1965): Allowed free trade of cars and car parts, because, let's be honest, both countries really love driving.
- NAFTA (1994) → USMCA (2020): A trade deal that basically made Canada, the U.S., and Mexico financially inseparable, like three kids stuck in a group project for eternity.

Today, the U.S. and Canada share one of the largest trade relationships in the world, exchanging over $600 billion in goods and services each year—making Canada the U.S.'s biggest customer (yes, bigger than China).

So while the U.S. and Canada may still argue over things like who invented basketball (it was a Canadian, but the U.S. perfected it), they're more economically intertwined than ever.

Cultural Exchanges: We're More Alike Than We Admit

Despite all the historical differences, the U.S. and Canada have always influenced each other culturally, thanks to:

- Hollywood: Canada provides the U.S. with some of its most famous actors (Ryan Reynolds, Jim Carrey, Keanu Reeves, Celine Dion—yes, she counts!).
- Music: You like Drake, Justin Bieber, and The Weeknd? You're welcome.
- Sports: Canadians brought hockey to the U.S., and in return, America gave Canada... the Buffalo Bills playing in Toronto sometimes.
- Fast Food: Tim Hortons is slowly invading the U.S., while McDonald's and Starbucks have long conquered Canada.

Ultimately, U.S. and Canadian cultures have blended so much that most people outside North America can't even tell us apart (seriously, just ask a European tourist).

Fun Fact:
The term "O.K." was popularized during the War of 1812, symbolizing "Old Kinderhook," a nickname for President Martin Van Buren. However, if Canada had won the war, we might all be saying "Eh.K." instead.

Final Thoughts: From Colonial Cousins to Economic Partners

So, what have we learned today?

- The U.S. and Canada started as British colonies but took very different paths.
- The U.S. tried (and failed) to conquer Canada in 1812, and Canadians never let them forget it.
- Despite past conflicts, the U.S. and Canada have built one of the strongest trade and cultural partnerships in the world.

- And most importantly: If Canada ever became a U.S. state, it wouldn't be that weird—because they already share half their economy, half their celebrities, and 100% of their sarcasm.

So, could Canada and the U.S. ever truly unite under one flag? Stay tuned, because in the next chapter, we'll dive into the political philosophies that keep them apart (or bring them closer together).

Political Philosophies:
Comparing Governance Model

Analyze the differences and similarities between Canadian and U.S. political systems.

Main Points and Objectives:
•   Parliamentary vs. Presidential Systems: Compare the structures of government and their implications for policy-making.
•   Federalism in Both Countries: Discuss how federal and provincial/state powers are allocated and exercised.
•   Party Systems: Examine the multi-party landscape in Canada versus the predominantly two-party system in the U.S.
•   Implications for Statehood: Consider how these political philosophies would mesh or clash in the event of unification.

Fun Fact: Canada's political parties often have more colorful names, like the Rhinoceros Party, which humorously advocated for promises it couldn't keep.

Would Canada's Political System Survive as a U.S. State, or Would It Melt Like a Popsicle in July?

The U.S. and Canada: Two Political Systems, One Long Border

If the United States and Canada were people, their political ideologies would be cousins who went to different colleges—one went to Harvard Law (strict constitutional originalist), and the other studied Political Science at the University of Toronto (believes in compromise, free healthcare, and apologizing when bumping into inanimate objects).

While the U.S. swears by its presidential system, Canada prefers parliamentary democracy—which, if you're unfamiliar, is basically democracy but with more polite arguments and far fewer filibusters.

So, let's compare the political structures, power divisions, and party landscapes to see how well (or how poorly) Canada's system would integrate into the United States if it became a state.

And, because I'm a professor with a dad-joke addiction, expect a few terrible puns along the way.

Parliamentary vs. Presidential Systems: Who Runs the Show?

The U.S. Presidential System: One Big Boss, Lots of Red Tape

The U.S. operates under a presidential system, meaning:

- The President is elected separately from Congress and serves as both head of state (symbolic leader) and head of government (policy enforcer).
- Congress (House & Senate) passes laws, but the President can veto them (and then Congress can veto the veto... it's like political tennis, but with filibusters).
- Presidents don't answer to Congress daily—they have fixed four-year terms (unless impeached, but that's a whole other drama).

Translation: The U.S. President has to fight tooth and nail to get things done unless their party controls both houses of Congress. Otherwise, governing can feel like running on a treadmill—lots of motion, but no movement.

Canada's Parliamentary System: A Team Effort (Mostly)

Canada's parliamentary democracy works a little differently:

- The Prime Minister (PM) is not directly elected by the people but is the leader of the party that wins the most seats in Parliament (imagine if the U.S. President were picked by Congress, not voters).
- If the PM's party has a majority, they control Parliament and can pass laws more easily.
- If they only have a minority, they must make deals with other parties to stay in power (Canadian politics = compromise or collapse).
- No fixed election dates! The Prime Minister can call an election whenever they think they can win—or get ousted by their own party and replaced mid-term (U.K. politics, but with more snow).

Translation: The Prime Minister can pass laws faster than a U.S. President if they have a majority, but if they don't, things get... messy.

Would This Work in a Canada-U.S. Merger?

Not easily! If Canada became a U.S. state, it would:

* Lose the Prime Minister position altogether (bye, PM!).
* Have to elect Governors and State Legislators, who would report to Washington, D.C.
* Have to get used to Presidents serving four-year terms no matter how unpopular they get (unlike Prime Ministers, who can be swapped out like hockey line changes).

* No more snap elections—Canadians would have to wait patiently like their southern neighbors.

Would Canadians be okay with this? Doubtful.

Federalism: Who Controls What?

Both Canada and the U.S. are federal systems, meaning power is divided between a central government and regional governments (states/provinces). But the balance of power between national and local governments differs significantly.

U.S. Federalism: More Power to the States
- Each U.S. state has its own governor, legislature, and courts.
- States control education, law enforcement, taxes, and even some healthcare policies.
- But Washington, D.C. still controls defense, currency, and foreign policy.

Some states (looking at you, Texas) like to push their autonomy to the limit, while others (hello, California!) enjoy their federal benefits.

Canadian Federalism: The Provinces Call the Shots
- Canadian provinces have even more power than U.S. states! They control education, healthcare, and even some taxation.
- The national government has limited influence over provincial affairs—which is why Quebec does its own thing (sometimes in French).
- Unlike U.S. states, provinces can't just leave the country on a whim (sorry, Alberta).

Would Canadian provinces be okay with losing power to Washington, D.C.?
Not likely.

Party Systems: A Political Buffet vs. A Two-Party Tug-of-War

The U.S.: Two-Party System
The U.S. is basically a two-party nation:
- Democrats (liberal, blue)
- Republicans (conservative, red)

Sure, there are independent candidates (shoutout to Bernie Sanders), but third parties rarely win major elections. It's a system where politics is more like a football game—two teams, one winner.

Canada: A Multi-Party Wonderland
Canada, on the other hand, has a smorgasbord of political parties:
- Liberal Party (center-left, red)
- Conservative Party (center-right, blue)
- New Democratic Party (NDP, progressive, orange)
- Bloc Québécois (separatists, French-speaking)
- Green Party (environmentalists, green)
- The Rhinoceros Party (satirical, mostly just here for fun)

If Canada became a U.S. state, its political parties would vanish overnight, forcing Canadians to choose between just two (cue dramatic music).

Would they enjoy that? Highly unlikely.

Fun Fact:

Canada has some of the strangest political party names in history, including:
- The Rhinoceros Party (which once promised to repeal the law of gravity).
- The Marijuana Party (focused on, well, marijuana).

- The Pirate Party (no actual pirates, just digital freedom advocates).

Try running for office in the U.S. under one of these names. Good luck!

Final Thoughts: Would Canada's Politics Survive in the U.S.?

If Canada ever became a U.S. state, it would mean:

No more Prime Ministers—just Governors and Senators reporting to Washington.
Provinces would lose some autonomy to the federal government.
Canadians would have to pick between just two political parties instead of five.
No more snap elections—just fixed four-year presidential terms.

Would Canadians accept this? Probably not without a LOT of maple syrup as compensation.

But hey, politics is about compromise, and if the U.S. and Canada can agree on hockey, fast food, and watching bad reality TV... maybe anything is possible.

| 4 |

Economic Entanglements:
Trade and Beyond

D elve into the deep economic connections between the two nations and the potential impact of statehood.

Main Points and Objectives:
- Trade Agreements: Review key agreements like NAFTA and USMCA and their outcomes.
- Cross-Border Investments: Highlight major sectors with significant bilateral investments.
- Labor Mobility: Discuss the movement of workers and professionals between the countries.
- Economic Pros and Cons of Statehood: Analyze potential economic benefits and drawbacks of integration.

Fun Fact: The U.S. and Canada are each other's largest trading partners, exchanging goods and services worth over $600 billion annually.

Would Merging Economies Create a Superpower or Just a Super Mess?

Canada and the U.S.: An Economic Bromance for the Ages

When it comes to economic partnerships, the United States and Canada are like a long-married couple who share bank accounts, business ventures, and the occasional disagreement over whose turn it is to take out the garbage (or in this case, set trade tariffs).

With over $600 billion in annual trade, these two nations are already financially linked tighter than a moose in a too-small sweater. But what if Canada officially joined the U.S.? Would it lead to economic prosperity, job creation, and financial harmony, or would it be a bureaucratic nightmare full of red tape, currency headaches, and disgruntled beaver mascots?

Grab your loonie, your toonie, and maybe a few U.S. dollars—it's time to dive into the economic entanglements of a U.S.-Canada merger.

Trade Agreements: The Economic Glue Between Two Giants

First, A Quick History of U.S.-Canada Trade Deals

Before Canada and the U.S. became economic BFFs, trade was a little... complicated. Picture two neighbors who wanted to share resources but kept haggling over fence height and whether or not to charge for borrowing the lawnmower.

Fast forward a few centuries, and we get a series of agreements that defined modern North American trade:

1. The Auto Pact (1965)
- This was like a joint custody agreement for car manufacturing.
- It ensured that U.S. and Canadian auto industries worked together instead of competing.

- The result? Cheaper cars and a ton of Canadian jobs in manufacturing.

2. NAFTA (1994) – The Deal That Changed Everything
- The North American Free Trade Agreement (NAFTA) created a huge economic zone between the U.S., Canada, and Mexico.
- It removed most tariffs, meaning goods could cross borders without extra taxes.
- Some loved it ("Free trade! More jobs! Lower prices!"), while others hated it ("Lost manufacturing jobs! Outsourcing! Globalization panic!").

3. USMCA (2020) – NAFTA 2.0, Now with More Drama
- After a few intense Twitter rants and heated negotiations, NAFTA was rebranded as the USMCA (United States-Mexico-Canada Agreement).
- Changes included tougher labor laws, auto manufacturing protections, and new digital trade rules.
- Basically, same trade deal, but with a fresh coat of political paint.

If Canada became a U.S. state, these agreements would become pointless—because suddenly, trade between the two would be domestic trade!

Would that be good? Bad? Confusing? Let's find out.

Cross-Border Investments: Where the Money Flows

The U.S. and Canada are already each other's largest investors, meaning:

- U.S. companies pour billions into Canada, especially in oil, energy, banking, and tech.

- Canadian firms invest billions in the U.S., from real estate to entertainment to doughnut shops (Tim Hortons, we see you).

Key Sectors Dominated by U.S.-Canada Investments:

1. Energy & Natural Resources – Canada exports oil and natural gas to the U.S. like it's an all-you-can-eat buffet.

2. Technology – Canada's tech hubs in Toronto, Vancouver, and Montreal are linked to Silicon Valley, creating a cross-border talent pipeline.

3. Banking – Canadian banks have major U.S. branches, while U.S. banks loan billions to Canadian businesses.

4. Entertainment – Half of your favorite "American" movies were filmed in Vancouver and Toronto, so if Canada became a state, Hollywood might just relocate north.

If Canada joined the U.S., all these foreign investment regulations would vanish overnight. But would that be a financial windfall or economic chaos?

Labor Mobility: Moving for Work—With or Without a Visa

Ever met a Canadian who works in the U.S. or an American who moved to Canada? That's because labor mobility between the two countries is already surprisingly fluid.

- There are over a million Canadians living in the U.S. right now.
- About 800,000 Americans live in Canada—mostly for jobs, healthcare, and the promise of maple syrup-infused citizenship.
- NAFTA (and later USMCA) made it easier for professionals to work across borders without crazy visa restrictions.

But if Canada became a state? No more visas needed! It would be as easy as moving from New York to Florida (except with fewer retirees and more moose).

Would this lead to a mass migration of workers? Would Americans flood into Canada for jobs? Would Canadians move south for the cheaper Big Macs?

We'd have to find out.

Economic Pros and Cons of Statehood

Like any major economic shift, a U.S.-Canada merger would come with opportunities AND serious headaches.

Economic Pros:
* No More Trade Barriers – No tariffs, no customs, no hassle.
* Stronger North American Economy – Combined GDP would be over $30 trillion (bye-bye, China).
* More Job Opportunities – Businesses could hire freely across the continent.
* Currency Stability – The U.S. dollar is stronger than the Canadian dollar, reducing inflation risks.

Economic Cons:
* Goodbye, Canadian Dollar – Canada's iconic loonie and toonie would be replaced by the U.S. dollar (which might make some Canadians cry into their Tim Hortons cups).
* Wage Disparities – Salaries are higher in some U.S. states than in Canada—could workers handle the transition?
* Rising Costs? – Would U.S. cost-of-living standards inflate Canadian prices? Would healthcare become less affordable?
* Political Clashes Over Resources – Who controls Alberta's oil? Would Washington dictate Canada's energy policy?

This isn't just an economic change—it's a fundamental shift in how money, labor, and business operate across borders.

Fun Fact:

The U.S. and Canada exchange over $600 billion in goods and services every year—making them each other's biggest customers. In other words, the economic bond is already so strong that Canada becoming a U.S. state wouldn't change much—except it would remove all the bureaucratic paperwork.

Final Thoughts: Would Merging Economies Work?

If Canada joined the U.S., it would:

Eliminate trade barriers overnight.
Dramatically increase economic power.
Allow millions of workers to move freely across borders.
Replace the Canadian dollar with the U.S. dollar (RIP, loonie).
Potentially create economic disputes over wages, cost of living, and industry regulations.

Would the economic benefits outweigh the risks? That's a question for economists, politicians, and probably an army of lawyers. But one thing's for sure: integrating two massive economies isn't like merging two coffee shops—it's more like fusing two planets.

Would the result be a superpower economy or an economic train wreck? Only time would tell.

| 5 |

Cultural Mosaic: Identity and Integration

Examine the cultural identities of both nations and the challenges of blending them.

Main Points and Objectives:
• National Identities: Explore what it means to be Canadian versus American.
• Cultural Institutions: Compare institutions like national holidays, sports, and arts.
• Integration Challenges: Discuss potential cultural clashes and synergies in a unified nation.
• Preservation of Heritage: Consider strategies to maintain cultural uniqueness post-integration.

Fun Fact: Canada's national sport is officially lacrosse, but ice hockey

Would Canada Keep Its Culture, or Would It Become North Montana?

Canada and the U.S.: Two Cultures, One Border, Infinite Stereotypes

Let's be honest—Americans and Canadians love stereotyping each other. Americans think of Canada as a winter wonderland full of maple syrup, hockey, and people who say "sorry" for no reason. Canadians, on the other hand, see the U.S. as a chaotic land of bald eagles, fast food, and extreme enthusiasm for the word "freedom."

But behind the jokes, both countries have rich, distinct cultures that shape their identities. So if Canada suddenly became a U.S. state (or several states), what would happen to its culture?

Would Thanksgiving move to November? Would Canadians have to pretend they like American football? Would Tim Hortons be forced to merge with Dunkin' Donuts?

Let's dive into the cultural entanglements of a U.S.-Canada merger, from national identities to sports rivalries, integration challenges, and the great battle over the letter "u" in words like "colour."

National Identities: What It Means to Be Canadian vs. American

If you ask a Canadian what it means to be Canadian, they'll likely answer, "Well, we're not American." Which is kind of like defining yourself by what you're not, but hey, whatever works.

But seriously, while the two countries share a lot in common, their national identities have developed in different ways over time.

What Defines Canadian Identity?
- Politeness – Canadians are famous for apologizing even when it's unnecessary (fun fact: there's an actual law in Canada stating that saying "sorry" in court is not an admission of guilt!).
- Multiculturalism – Canada embraces cultural diversity as a defining feature, and has fewer debates over immigration than the U.S.

- Peacekeeping Over Militarism – While the U.S. has the world's largest military, Canada is known for diplomacy, peacekeeping, and using "strongly worded letters" instead of missiles.

- Social Policies – Canadians are generally more accepting of public healthcare, stricter gun laws, and stronger government services compared to their American counterparts.

- French Language & Quebec – Canada has two official languages (English and French), with Quebec being the "we'll leave if you annoy us" province.

What Defines American Identity?

- Individualism & Patriotism – Americans have more flags per square mile than any other country and love the idea of "picking yourself up by your bootstraps" (which is confusing because most modern boots don't even have straps).

- Freedom as a Core Value – Freedom of speech, freedom to bear arms, freedom to put bacon on everything—Americans take their liberties seriously.

- Sports Obsession – The U.S. has the NFL, NBA, MLB, and March Madness—basically, a major sporting event every week of the year.

- Bigger Is Better Mentality – From cars to fast food portions to skyscrapers, Americans believe in going big or going home.

- Hollywood & Pop Culture – The U.S. dominates the world's film, music, and entertainment industries, exporting American culture globally.

If Canada became a U.S. state, would it lose these defining traits, or would it carve out a uniquely "Canadian-American" identity?

Cultural Institutions: National Holidays, Sports, and the Arts

What happens when you merge two cultures with different holidays, national sports, and traditions? A lot of interesting negotiations.

Holidays: A Scheduling Nightmare
One of the first arguments in a U.S.-Canada merger would be over holiday dates.

- Thanksgiving: Canada celebrates in October, the U.S. in November. Would Canadians have to wait an extra month for turkey?
- Independence Day vs. Canada Day: July 1st or July 4th? Would a merged country just call it "North American Fireworks Weekend"?
- Boxing Day: Canadians get December 26th off, while Americans only get leftover turkey. Would this holiday be saved or scrapped?
- Victoria Day vs. Memorial Day: Both are in May, but one honors the British monarchy (yikes). Would America allow this one to survive?

Sports: The Great Hockey vs. Football Debate
Americans love football. Canadians love hockey. This is non-negotiable.

If Canada became part of the U.S.:
- Would the NFL replace the CFL? (The Canadian Football League has only three downs—would Americans even understand it?)
- Would NHL teams get more funding than the NBA? (Sorry, basketball fans, Canada has priorities.)
- Would the Stanley Cup be considered an "American" trophy? (Cue Canadian outrage.)

Fun Fact: Canada's official national sport is lacrosse, not hockey. Shocking, right? But don't worry, Canadians still treat hockey like a religion.

Integration Challenges: The U in Colour and the Fahrenheit Fiasco

Blending two cultures isn't just about big things like sports and politics—it's also about the little things that drive people crazy when they change.

Language Differences:
- Canada spells words with extra "U"s (colour, honour, neighbour). Would Americans force Canada to spell things "correctly"?
- Would Quebec demand French be an official U.S. language? (France is watching closely... ◈)
- Would Americans finally understand what "toque" means? (It's a winter hat. You're welcome.)

Measurement Confusion:
- Canada uses the metric system. The U.S. does not. Would Canadians have to give up kilometers and Celsius?
- Would they finally start measuring their height in feet instead of centimeters?
- Would Americans have to convert their temperatures to Celsius? (Spoiler: No. The U.S. is very committed to Fahrenheit.)

Driving Rules:
- Speed limits would switch from km/h to mph. Expect a few Canadians getting speeding tickets.
- Would road signs switch to "YIELD" instead of "MERGE"?
- Would Canadians finally get used to turning right on red?

Preservation of Heritage: Keeping Canada Canadian (Even as a U.S. State)

If Canada joined the U.S., could it preserve its unique culture?

Potential strategies:

* "Cultural Protection Laws" – Quebec already protects its language, so why not extend this to Canadian traditions and institutions?

* "Regional Autonomy" – Canada could keep its own laws on language, media, and even public services like healthcare (at least, in theory).

* "Special Status in Congress" – Could Canada's former provinces have extra representation to protect their interests?

Could Canada be the first U.S. state (or states) with an official bilingual policy?

Final Thoughts: Can Culture Survive Statehood?

If Canada became a U.S. state, expect:
* Major holiday and sports debates.
* Arguments over spelling and measurement systems.
* Cultural preservation efforts to maintain Canadian identity.
* A fierce fight to keep hockey as a top sport.

Would Canadians be willing to trade their cultural independence for statehood benefits? Or would the phrase "Sorry, we prefer being our own country" win the day?

| 6 |

Pros of Canada Joining the U.S.

The economic, political, and strategic benefits of Canada becoming a U.S. state.

Key Topics:
- Economic benefits: stronger trade ties, access to U.S. federal funding
- Military and defense improvements: NATO alignment, combined military power
- Political stability: less political fragmentation

Fun Fact: If Canada became a U.S. state, it would instantly become the largest U.S. state by land area, overtaking Alaska!

More Trade, More Power, More Maple Syrup?

Would Canada Be Better Off as a U.S. State?

If you ask a Canadian about joining the U.S., you'll probably hear, "Thanks, but no thanks, eh?" But what if we set aside national pride, metric system loyalty, and an undying love for the Queen (well, King now) and looked at this purely from a strategic perspective?

Could statehood bring more economic growth, stronger military alliances, and political stability? Would Canadians benefit financially from U.S. tax structures, government programs, and investment opportunities?

Or—and hear me out here—would Canada just be the biggest, coldest Florida? ◈ ◈

Let's break down the strongest arguments in favor of statehood, from economics to defense to political stability, and see if Canada really would come out ahead.

1. Economic Benefits: The Dollar, The Jobs, The Trade Deals

Stronger Trade Ties – Goodbye, Tariffs!
Canada and the U.S. already trade over $600 billion in goods and services annually (that's more money than the GDP of Sweden, just floating across the border in trucks full of lumber, oil, and—yes—maple syrup).

If Canada joined the U.S., trade would become domestic commerce—meaning:
* No more tariffs on exports and imports.
* Lower business costs for Canadian companies selling to the U.S.
* Seamless supply chains for industries like auto manufacturing and agriculture.

Essentially, Canadian businesses could operate without restrictions across all 50—er, 51+—states, making expansion and profits far easier.

Access to U.S. Federal Funding

Ever heard the phrase "follow the money"? Well, the U.S. spends a lot of it—on infrastructure, defense, education, and healthcare (even if that last one is a bit of a mess).

If Canada became a state, it would gain access to massive amounts of U.S. federal funding, including:

Highway and transportation grants (hello, bullet trains?)

Disaster relief funds (for when an angry moose destroys a town, obviously)

Education and research funding (more money for top universities)

Agricultural subsidies (good news for wheat farmers in the Prairies!)

Would this make Canadian life better? Maybe. Would it mean higher government spending per capita? Absolutely.

A More Stable Currency – The End of the Canadian Dollar?

Let's face it: the U.S. dollar is more globally influential than the Canadian dollar (sorry, loonie lovers).

If Canada joined the U.S., the loonie and toonie would disappear—replaced by American greenbacks.

Pros:

* No more exchange rate headaches when traveling to the U.S.

* Stronger global purchasing power for Canadians.

* Easier international trade (no more conversions).

Cons:

* Goodbye, uniquely Canadian money (so long, bills with hockey players and beavers).

* U.S. inflation would affect Canada directly (cue mild economic panic).

* Would Canada lose financial independence?

It's a trade-off—but for those who hate exchange rates, it's a win.

2. Military & Defense: Bigger, Better, More Funded

Stronger Military Defense – The Ultimate Upgrade
Canada is known for peacekeeping, while the U.S. is known for having the largest military budget on Earth (seriously, it's bigger than the next nine countries combined).

Currently, Canada spends about 1.4% of GDP on defense.
The U.S. spends over 3.5%—which is like Canada but on steroids.

If Canada became a U.S. state, its military would gain access to:
* More funding for defense technology
* Better equipment and resources (goodbye, outdated fighter jets!)
* Greater homeland security support

Basically, Canada would instantly become more secure—because let's be real, nobody invades a U.S. state (except maybe tourists from Florida).

Stronger Border Control (or No Border at All!)
- Right now, Canada spends billions on border security—but if it became part of the U.S., the border would disappear.
- This would make travel and business easier (no more long waits at customs!), but also mean more security integration with U.S. agencies.

Would Canadians be okay with American-style border policies? That's another debate.

3. Political Stability: Less Fragmentation, More Representation

One of the biggest concerns in Canadian politics is regional division—Alberta and Quebec often disagree on policies, while the Atlantic provinces feel neglected.

If Canada became part of the U.S., these internal divides might actually become less of an issue.

Why?
* Equal Senate Representation: Every U.S. state gets two Senators, meaning Alberta wouldn't have to fight Ottawa for attention—it would fight in Washington instead!
* More House Representatives: Canada would gain dozens of seats in Congress, giving it more influence on national policy.
* No More Separatist Movements: Would Quebec finally stop threatening to leave if it became a U.S. state? (Doubtful, but hey, worth a shot.)

Basically, Canada's provinces would become more powerful than ever—but only if they're okay with playing by U.S. political rules.

Fun Fact: Canada Would Overtake Alaska as the Largest U.S. State

Right now, Alaska is the biggest U.S. state—but if Canada joined, it would immediately become the largest by land area (sorry, Alaska, you had a good run).

- Canada's total land area: 3.85 million square miles
- Alaska's land area: 663,000 square miles
- Texas? Not even close.

If all of Canada became one state, it would be bigger than the next three largest states combined! (Talk about bragging rights!).

Final Thoughts: Would Statehood Be Worth It?

The Pros, Summarized:
* Stronger trade ties = more business opportunities.
* More U.S. funding for infrastructure and research.
* No more currency exchange headaches.
* Better military defense and border security.
* More political representation in Washington.

Of course, the big question remains:
Would Canadians accept giving up their independent identity for these benefits?

(Spoiler alert: Probably not without a lot of negotiations and a national referendum.)

But on paper, the U.S. and Canada are already so closely linked that merging wouldn't be as crazy as it sounds—at least, economically and strategically.

The real challenge? Convincing Canadians that life as a U.S. state would actually be better.

(And let's be honest, that might take more than just economic arguments—it might require unlimited free healthcare and a lifetime supply of Tim Hortons.)

| 7 |

Cons of Canada Joining the U.S.

The economic, cultural, and political downsides.

Key Topics:
- Loss of Canadian identity
- Fear of U.S. partisanship infecting Canadian politics
- Economic risks: potential tax hikes, higher healthcare costs

Fun Fact: Canadians love their "free" healthcare. 60% of Canadians say they wouldn't give it up for anything—even if it meant winning free Tim Hortons coffee for life!

Would Canadians Trade Their Maple Leaf for Stars and Stripes? Not So Fast...

Would Statehood Ruin Canada?

Last chapter, we looked at all the logical reasons Canada might want to join the U.S.—more trade, stronger defense, and better access to government funding.

But logic doesn't always win over hearts. (If it did, people wouldn't order pineapple on pizza.)

For many Canadians, the idea of giving up their independent identity to become part of the U.S. is about as appealing as finding a moose in your living room—unexpected, alarming, and bound to create a mess.

So before we start designing a new U.S. flag with an extra maple leaf, let's examine the biggest reasons why Canada might reject statehood faster than a hockey goalie swatting away a slap shot.

1. Loss of Canadian Identity: Would "Canada" Even Exist Anymore?

Let's Be Real—Canadians Take Their Identity Very Seriously
Canada isn't just "America with colder weather." It has a distinct history, culture, and way of life that Canadians are deeply proud of.

If Canada became a U.S. state, it would:
Lose its own flag—goodbye, red and white maple leaf.
No longer have a Prime Minister—just a governor answering to Washington, D.C.
No more separate national holidays—July 1st (Canada Day)? Replaced with July 4th!
Goodbye, British ties—Canada still recognizes the British monarchy (even if most Canadians don't send King Charles Christmas cards).

Could Canada Keep Its Culture Within the U.S.?
The U.S. has a habit of absorbing cultures (see: the entire history of Hollywood). If Canada joined, would its unique quirks get swallowed up by American influence?

Would people still sing O Canada? Would the world still recognize Canada as "the nice country"? Or would it just be…Minnesota but bigger?

For many Canadians, the thought of losing their national identity is a deal-breaker.

2. Fear of U.S. Partisanship Infecting Canada

Canada's Political Climate Is… Milder
The U.S. is known for its hyper-partisan political battles—think of it like a never-ending boxing match between two heavyweight champions who refuse to tap out.

Canada? More like a polite debate club where everyone shakes hands afterward.

If Canada became a state:
- Would U.S. partisanship seep into Canadian politics?
- Would Canadians be forced to pick a side in the two-party system?
- Would issues like gun control and healthcare become partisan wars instead of settled policies?

Imagine U.S. News Networks Covering Canada
Right now, Canadian political coverage is calm and policy-focused. But if Canada joined the U.S., suddenly you'd hear:

- "BREAKING NEWS: ALBERTA FLIPS REPUBLICAN!"
- "QUEBEC LEADS NATIONAL PUSH FOR FREE HEALTHCARE—AGAIN!"
- "MAPLE SYRUP PRICES SKYROCKET AFTER NEW TRADE WAR WITH VERMONT!"

For many Canadians, this alone is enough to say no thanks.

3. Economic Risks: Higher Taxes, More Healthcare Costs

Canadians Pay Higher Taxes, but Get More in Return
Canada has higher taxes than the U.S., but in exchange, it gets:
* Free healthcare for all
* Cheaper college tuition
* Stronger social safety nets

In the U.S., the system is different:
Lower taxes—but higher costs for services
Private healthcare means higher out-of-pocket expenses
More economic inequality

What Happens to Healthcare?
The biggest fear Canadians have about statehood is losing their healthcare system.

- Right now, every Canadian has free access to hospitals, doctors, and prescriptions.
- In the U.S., healthcare is private, expensive, and confusing.
- A single hospital visit in the U.S. can cost more than a month's rent.

Would Canada be forced into the U.S. system? Would free healthcare disappear?
Or would Canadians demand that the U.S. adopt universal healthcare instead?

(Spoiler: Americans might object to that last one.)

For many Canadians, free healthcare is non-negotiable—so if statehood means losing it, expect the answer to be a hard no.

4. Quebec Would Absolutely Lose It

Would Quebec Even Agree to This?
Let's be honest—Quebec already has a complicated relationship with Canada. The province has nearly separated multiple times, and it fiercely protects its French language and culture.

If Canada became a U.S. state, Quebec would:
Lose its ability to enforce French as an official language.
Be ruled by Washington instead of Ottawa.
Likely launch a full-fledged independence movement overnight.

In other words—Quebec might not just reject U.S. statehood. It might reject Canada altogether.

Could the U.S. handle a secession crisis before even finishing Canada's onboarding paperwork? Probably not.

5. Would Canada Just Be… Another Northern State?

Would the Rest of the U.S. Even Notice?
Let's say Canada becomes the 51st state. Would Americans suddenly take an interest in Canadian culture and history?

Or would Canada fade into the background, becoming just "America, but colder"?

Think about other large U.S. states like Alaska or Montana—how often do they dominate national conversations?

Would Canadians be okay becoming just another star on the flag, rather than a sovereign nation that punches above its weight in global diplomacy?

For many, being a big fish in a small pond (Canada) is better than being a small fish in a huge ocean (the U.S.).

Fun Fact: Healthcare vs. Tim Hortons

A survey found that 60% of Canadians would rather keep their free healthcare than get free Tim Hortons coffee for life.

This proves two things:
1. Canadians really, really love healthcare.
2. Even Tim Hortons has its limits.

Final Thoughts: Why Canada Would Likely Say No

For all the logical economic and security benefits of joining the U.S., Canada would have to sacrifice a LOT:

Losing national identity and sovereignty
Getting pulled into U.S. partisanship and political fights
Risking their beloved healthcare system
Potential Quebec separatism
Becoming "just another state" instead of a globally recognized country

Would any of these be worth it just to save money on trade or military defense?

(Most Canadians would probably say no faster than you can say "Sorry, but we're good, eh?")

And that's why, despite centuries of close U.S.-Canada relations, Canada is likely to remain its own country for the foreseeable future.

(At least, unless the U.S. offers free hockey tickets to sweeten the deal.)

| 8 |

Political Representation

If Canada became a U.S. state (or multiple states), how would it be represented in Congress?

This chapter explores how many Senators and Representatives Canada would get, how its political landscape would shift American politics, and what it would mean for future elections.

Main Points & Objectives:
- How Many Senators and Representatives Would Canada Get?
- Each U.S. state gets 2 Senators—would Canada have just 2, or more if divided into multiple states?
- Representation in the House of Representatives is based on population—Canada's 39 million people could mean 50+ new Representatives!
- How Would Canadian Political Ideologies Fit?
- Would Canada's generally liberal political culture create more Democratic-leaning states?
- Would conservative provinces like Alberta shift the U.S. Republican base?
- Impact on the U.S. Electoral College
- Canada's electoral votes would shift the balance of power in presidential elections.
- Could this permanently favor one political party?

- Would Canada Have Influence or Be Overpowered?

- As a U.S. state, Canada would lose its Prime Minister and only have a fraction of influence compared to the power it has as a sovereign nation.

- Would Canadians accept this trade-off?

Fun Fact: If Canada joined as one state, it would instantly become the largest U.S. state by population after California! But if it were divided into multiple states, it could have more electoral votes than Texas!

Would Canada Run Washington, or Just Be Another Star on the Flag?

Welcome to Congress, Canada! Here's Your Seat... or 50?

If Canada became a U.S. state (or, realistically, several states), one of the biggest questions would be: how much political power would it actually have in Washington, D.C.?

Would Canada dominate Congress, turning the U.S. into an honorary branch of the Great White North? Or would it be politically overshadowed, like a small-town mayor trying to influence national policy?

Let's dive into the numbers, the politics, and—of course—the fun of imagining what "Senator from Saskatchewan" would sound like in a U.S. political debate.

1. How Many Senators and Representatives Would Canada Get?

The Senate: Would Canada Have 2 Senators or 20?
- Every U.S. state gets two Senators, no matter its population.
- Alaska (pop. 700,000) has 2 Senators, and so does California (pop. 39 million).
- So if Canada became one giant state, it would only get 2 Senators—the same as Wyoming, which has fewer people than Ottawa!

That's a bad deal for Canada.

Solution? More Than One State.
Instead of one giant state, Canada could split into multiple states, each with its own Senators.

- If each Canadian province became its own state, that would be 10 new U.S. states (not counting the 3 territories).
- That's 20 new Senators!
- If territories like Yukon, Northwest Territories, and Nunavut got statehood too, we're talking 26 Senators total.

That would seriously shake up the U.S. Senate, giving Canada massive influence.

Fun thought: Would Canada's new states team up in the Senate to protect Canadian-style policies? Imagine the Maple Leaf Caucus demanding free healthcare for everyone!

The House of Representatives: Canada Could Outnumber Texas!
Unlike the Senate, the House of Representatives is based on population.

Canada's population: 39 million people
Each U.S. Representative represents about 760,000 people

So, if Canada were one state...
- It would get about 50 Representatives—instantly making it one of the most powerful voting blocs in Congress!
- Only California (52 seats) would have more influence.

If Canada Were Multiple States?
- Ontario alone (14.5 million people) would get about 19 Representatives!
- Quebec (8.5 million) would get 11 Representatives.
- Even smaller provinces like Nova Scotia and Manitoba would get 3-4 seats each.

In total, if each province were its own state, Canada could add over 70 new House seats—potentially outnumbering Texas!

Would Congress be ready for that kind of Canadian invasion?

2. How Would Canadian Political Ideologies Fit in the U.S.?

Would Canada Lean Democratic or Republican?

Canada is generally more liberal than the U.S., but not every province thinks the same way.

Liberal-leaning provinces (Democratic-style politics):
- Quebec, British Columbia, Ontario, Nova Scotia – Strong on social programs, environmental policies, and healthcare.
- Would likely send mostly Democratic Representatives to Congress.

Conservative-leaning provinces (Republican-style politics):
- Alberta, Saskatchewan, Manitoba – Big on oil, low taxes, and strong skepticism of government overreach.
- Would likely send more Republican Representatives to Congress.

Wild card: Would Alberta become the Texas of the North? Would Quebec lobby for more federal programs?

Regardless, Canada's addition would shift the entire U.S. political landscape.

3. Impact on the U.S. Electoral College

Here's where things get REALLY interesting.

- The Electoral College decides U.S. presidential elections based on a state's number of Senators + Representatives.
- If Canada became one big state, it would get 50-55 electoral votes—more than Florida (30) or New York (28)!
- If each province became a state, Canada could control over 100 electoral votes—making it one of the biggest power players in presidential elections.

Would This Permanently Tip the Balance for One Party?

- If Canada votes mostly Democratic? The Republican Party might never win a presidential election again.

- If provinces like Alberta go Republican? It could create new battleground states.

Imagine a future election where candidates are campaigning in Toronto, Vancouver, and Montreal!

4. Would Canada Have Influence or Be Overpowered?

One concern Canadians would have is whether they'd actually have a voice or just become a giant Rhode Island—technically represented, but politically irrelevant.

Pros:
* More seats in Congress than almost any other U.S. state!
* Major influence over presidential elections.
* More federal funding and political power than before.

Cons:
* No more Prime Minister—only Governors and Representatives.
* Less autonomy compared to being an independent nation.
* Would have to deal with U.S. political drama full-time.

Would Canadians really want to trade their independent voice in the world for a fraction of influence in Washington, D.C.?

Fun Fact: Canada Would Become the Second-Largest U.S. Voting Bloc!

If Canada joined as one state, it would:
- Be the second-most powerful state in the Electoral College (after California).

- Control more House seats than Florida or New York.

If it joined as multiple states, it could become the single largest voting bloc in Congress—more powerful than Texas, Florida, and California combined!

Final Thoughts: Would Canada's Political Power Be Worth the Trade-Off?

Biggest Wins:
* Huge influence in the House of Representatives.
* More power in presidential elections.
* Stronger say over national policies.

Biggest Risks:
* Losing an independent voice in global politics.
* Quebec and Alberta would probably fight about everything.
* Would have to participate in the madness of U.S. elections.

Would Canadians be willing to trade their Prime Minister for Senators and Representatives?

Would Washington be ready for 100+ new Canadian politicians demanding universal healthcare and better hockey coverage on ESPN?

One thing is certain: If Canada joined the U.S., it wouldn't be a quiet, polite addition. It would be a political game-changer.

| 9 |

Healthcare Systems

One of the biggest concerns for Canadians is healthcare—would they lose their beloved universal system and be forced into the privatized U.S. model?

This chapter compares healthcare policies and explores what would happen in a statehood scenario.

Main Points & Objectives:
- How Does Canadian Healthcare Work?
  - Single-payer system—funded by taxes, everyone has access.
  - Lower drug prices, free emergency care, no medical bankruptcy.
- How Does U.S. Healthcare Work?
  - Privatized system—insurance-based, employer-driven.
  - Expensive medical costs, lack of universal coverage.
  - The Affordable Care Act (ACA/Obamacare) vs. Canada's system.
- Would Canada Keep Its Healthcare Model as a U.S. State?
  - Would provinces negotiate keeping their own system (like Massachusetts' healthcare reform)?
  - Could a hybrid model emerge?
- How Would This Affect Americans?

- If Canada joined, would Americans push for universal healthcare nationwide?
- Would U.S. insurance companies fight against statehood to prevent healthcare reform?

Fun Fact: A trip to the emergency room in Toronto costs $0. In the U.S., an ambulance ride alone can cost $1,000+—Canadians would definitely not be happy about that change!

Would Canadians Survive the U.S. Healthcare System? Or Would Americans Demand a Canadian Upgrade?

Welcome to the Healthcare Battle Royale

If there's one thing that scares Canadians more than an American-sized portion of poutine, it's the idea of losing their universal healthcare and getting tossed into the chaotic world of U.S. medical billing codes, surprise hospital bills, and insurance premiums that cost more than rent.

Ask any Canadian what they love about their country, and "free healthcare" is likely in the top three—right next to hockey and Tim Hortons.

So what happens if Canada joins the United States?

- Would Canada be forced to adopt America's privatized, employer-based system?
- Could Canadians negotiate keeping their universal healthcare?
- Would Americans finally demand universal care for themselves after seeing how much better Canada has it?

Let's compare how the two systems work, what would happen if they merged, and whether this could turn into the world's most awkward political healthcare debate.

1. How Does Canadian Healthcare Work?

The Basics: A Single-Payer Dreamland
Canada operates on a single-payer, publicly funded system—which means:

* All essential medical care is free at the point of service.
* Funded by taxes, so everyone contributes.
* No medical bankruptcies (a phrase that doesn't even exist in Canada).
* Lower drug prices (because the government negotiates prices).

Need an ambulance? Free.
Emergency room visit? Free.
Check-up, surgery, cancer treatment? Free.

The only thing that isn't covered? Prescription drugs, dental, and vision—but most Canadians have cheap supplemental insurance for that.

Fun Fact: Canadian doctors still earn great salaries! The government pays hospitals directly, but doctors operate as private businesses and bill the government for services rendered.

2. How Does U.S. Healthcare Work?

The Basics: A Complex, Expensive Puzzle
Unlike Canada, the U.S. healthcare system is mostly privatized, meaning:

* You need insurance to afford care.

* Insurance is mostly tied to employment.

* Even with insurance, there are co-pays, deductibles, and out-of-pocket costs.

* Without insurance? Be prepared for bankruptcy-level medical bills.

Need an ambulance? That'll be $1,000+.

Emergency room visit? Could cost anywhere from $500 to $50,000.

Cancer treatment? That'll be your life savings, please.

Obamacare (The Affordable Care Act) – The U.S. Attempt at Reform

- Expanded Medicaid for lower-income Americans.

- Created online marketplaces for private insurance.

- Required everyone to have insurance (until that mandate was removed).

- Still doesn't cover everyone—and still expensive.

Fun Fact: The average monthly cost of U.S. health insurance for a family is about $1,200 per month (that's enough for a first-class flight to Europe every month).

3. Would Canada Keep Its Healthcare Model as a U.S. State?

Now, let's get to the big question: Would Canada have to ditch its free healthcare and join the U.S. system, or could it keep things as they are?

Option 1: Keep Universal Healthcare (Like Massachusetts Did)

- Massachusetts has a state-run healthcare system that existed before the ACA.

- Could Canada negotiate a deal where it keeps its own system, similar to how some U.S. states have unique healthcare laws?

- Maybe! But this would require serious negotiations in Washington.

Option 2: A Hybrid System?

- Could Canada remain part of U.S. healthcare but keep its public funding model?

- Maybe Canada could set up a regional system where the federal government still funds it—kind of like a Medicare-for-all test state.

- But would Americans in other states demand the same?

Option 3: Forced Into the U.S. System (Disaster Scenario for Canadians)

- If Washington insists that all U.S. states follow the same healthcare model, Canada might have no choice.

- Canadians would have to buy private insurance, deal with out-of-pocket costs, and possibly lose their government-funded care altogether.

- Expect riots in the streets of Toronto if this happens.

If this is the case, expect Canadian statehood to FAIL at the voting booth.

4. How Would This Affect Americans?

Now, let's flip the question: If Canada kept its healthcare, would Americans start demanding the same?

Could Canada Be the Model That Pushes the U.S. to Universal Healthcare?

- Millions of Americans already support universal healthcare—but Congress has resisted major reform.

- If Canada joins the U.S. and keeps its public system, wouldn't Americans in other states demand the same?
- Could Canada be the "test case" that finally shifts U.S. healthcare?

Insurance companies would panic.

Pharmaceutical companies would panic.

But regular Americans? They might start asking, "Wait... why don't we have this?"

This could be one of the biggest unintended consequences of Canadian statehood—America accidentally adopting universal healthcare because the new Canadian states demand it.

5. Would U.S. Insurance Companies Try to Block Canadian Statehood?

Let's be real—big healthcare corporations have a LOT of influence in Washington.

Would the U.S. healthcare industry fight against Canadian statehood?

Would they lobby to force Canada into privatization?

Would Americans start protesting for healthcare reform?

If Canada joins but refuses to give up free healthcare, expect big-money lobbying battles in Congress like never before.

Fun Fact: In the U.S., the healthcare industry spends more on lobbying than any other sector—about $700 million per year.

If Canada's universal system threatens U.S. corporate profits, expect a massive legal and political fight to stop Canadian-style healthcare from spreading.

Final Thoughts: Healthcare Could Make or Break Statehood

If Canada became a U.S. state, the biggest political fight wouldn't be over trade, or even representation—it would be over healthcare.

What's at Stake?
* Could Canada keep its system? (Possible, but tough.)
* Would Americans demand universal care, too? (Very likely!)
* Would insurance companies fight statehood? (Almost definitely.)

For many Canadians, free healthcare is a deal-breaker. If statehood means losing it, statehood is dead on arrival.

But if Canada could keep it and push the U.S. toward reform? That might be the biggest benefit of all.

So, would healthcare be the reason Canada never joins the U.S.?

Stay tuned—because next, we're talking about military and defense, and whether Canada needs the U.S. Army or if a moose militia would be enough.

| 10 |

Military and Defense

C anada and the U.S. are strong military allies, but if Canada became a state, its independent military policies would change. Would Canada benefit from U.S. military spending, or would it lose control over its own defense?

Main Points & Objectives:
- How Does Canada's Military Compare to the U.S.?
- Canada has a much smaller military, focusing on peacekeeping rather than interventionism.
- The U.S. has the largest military in the world, with bases across the globe.
- Would Canada Lose Military Sovereignty?
- As a state, Canada couldn't make its own defense decisions anymore—Washington, D.C. would control everything.
- Would Canadians be okay with joining U.S. foreign wars?
- Military Spending: Would Canada Benefit or Lose Out?
- Canada currently spends far less on its military compared to the U.S.
- Could Canadian industries benefit from increased defense contracts?
- Would U.S. military presence increase in Canada, including more military bases?
- Would NATO and NORAD Policies Change?

- Canada and the U.S. already work together under NORAD (North American Aerospace Defense Command).
- Would Canada gain or lose strategic importance?

Fun Fact: Canada has no nuclear weapons and prohibits them on its soil—but as a U.S. state, would that change? Could Canada suddenly have nuclear missiles stationed in Alberta or Quebec?

Would Canada Gain Security... or Just Become America's Northern Military Outpost?

Would Canada Keep Control of Its Own Military, or Would Washington Call the Shots?

When you think of Canadian defense, you probably picture peacekeepers, Mounties, and that one time Canada "accidentally" invaded the U.S. (true story—more on that later).

Now, think of U.S. military power—a massive global force with more aircraft carriers than most countries have planes, a Pentagon the size of a small city, and a defense budget bigger than the GDP of most nations.

So, if Canada became a U.S. state, what happens to its military identity?

- Would Canada still have control over its own forces?
- Would it benefit from American military spending?
- Or would it just become another cog in the U.S. war machine?

Let's break it down—because while Canada and the U.S. are best friends in defense, joining forces might come with unexpected consequences.

1. How Does Canada's Military Compare to the U.S.?

Canada's Military: Small but Mighty (and Very, Very Cold)
Canada has a professional, highly trained military, but it's much smaller than the U.S. in both size and budget.

- Active Personnel: ~68,000
- Reserves: ~27,000
- Defense Budget: ~$26 billion
- Military Focus: Peacekeeping, Arctic defense, and disaster relief

Canada's main defense priorities are:
* Protecting its own territory (which is mostly snow and moose).
* Defending the Arctic from potential threats (mostly Russia).
* Peacekeeping missions with the UN (Canada loves diplomacy).
* Working with the U.S. and NATO (because having strong friends is smart).

The U.S. Military: A Global Superpower with a Bigger Budget Than Anyone Else
The U.S. military is, well... big. Very big.

- Active Personnel: ~1.3 million
- Reserves: ~800,000
- Defense Budget: ~$877 billion (Yes, you read that right.)
- Military Focus: Global intervention, deterrence, and maintaining 750+ military bases worldwide.

While Canada sees itself as a peacekeeper, the U.S. sees itself as the world's policeman (or at least, the guy who owns all the security cameras and a really big baton).

So, what happens if Canada joins the U.S.? Does it keep its peaceful military identity, or does it get absorbed into America's global strategy?

2. Would Canada Lose Military Sovereignty?

If Canada became a U.S. state, it would no longer have an independent military—its forces would be absorbed into the U.S. Army, Navy, Air Force, Marines, and Space Force (yes, Space Force is real).

Biggest Consequences for Canada:
* No more independent foreign policy. Canada couldn't say "Nah, we'll sit this one out" when the U.S. decides to intervene somewhere.
* No more Canadian-controlled deployments. Washington would decide where Canadian soldiers go.
* Would Canadians be okay fighting in U.S. wars? Many Canadians see their military as defensive, while the U.S. engages in global conflicts regularly.

Fun Fact: The last time Canada and the U.S. were in direct military conflict? The War of 1812—when Canada successfully defended itself from an American invasion. Since then, it's been mostly smooth sailing.

3. Military Spending: Would Canada Benefit or Lose Out?

One huge upside to U.S. statehood? Way more military funding.

What Canada Would Gain:
Access to the world's largest defense budget. Canada's military spending is only ~3% of the U.S. budget—imagine what it could do with billions more in resources!
Better military technology and infrastructure. More funding = better equipment, research, and Arctic defense systems.

More defense contracts for Canadian companies. Canada already produces top-tier aircraft, ships, and weapons—a U.S. merger could mean more money for Canadian defense industries.

What Canada Would Lose:

* No more control over its own defense budget. Washington would decide how much money goes where.

* More U.S. military bases on Canadian soil. This could be a deal-breaker for Canadians who don't want to see a McDonald's and a U.S. Air Force base next to Niagara Falls.

* Canada might be forced to spend more on defense. Right now, Canada spends only 1.4% of its GDP on the military—the U.S. might demand at least 2-3% like NATO requires.

Would Canadians want to spend more on weapons instead of healthcare, education, and snowplows?

4. Would NATO and NORAD Policies Change?

NORAD: The U.S.-Canada Defense Partnership That Already Exists

Did you know that Canada and the U.S. already defend North America together through NORAD (North American Aerospace Defense Command)?

- NORAD tracks all air and missile threats to North America (so if Santa Claus enters restricted airspace, we know).

- It's the only binational military agreement of its kind in the world—showing just how close U.S.-Canada defense ties already are.

Fun Fact: The U.S. and Canada also have a secret bunker complex deep inside Cheyenne Mountain, Colorado where NORAD operations take place. (If the world ever ends, expect a lot of Mounties in Colorado.)

Would NATO Be Affected?

- Canada is a founding member of NATO (the North Atlantic Treaty Organization).

- If Canada became a U.S. state, its voice in NATO would disappear—because it wouldn't be a separate country anymore.

- Would Europe be okay with that? Canada is seen as a diplomatic, stabilizing force in NATO. Losing that could shift power toward the more aggressive side of the alliance.

Would NATO become even more dominated by the U.S. without Canada's influence?

5. Would Canada Get Nukes?

Canada does not have nuclear weapons. It's part of an international treaty that prohibits nukes on its soil.

But if Canada became a U.S. state… would that change?

- Could the U.S. place nuclear weapons in Alberta, Saskatchewan, or Quebec?

- Would Canada have a say in where U.S. missiles are deployed?

- Would Canadians be okay with being part of America's nuclear strategy?

Fun Fact: During the Cold War, the U.S. tried to get Canada to host nuclear weapons. Canada said, "No thanks, eh."

If Canada became a state, it might not have a choice anymore.

Final Thoughts: Would Canada's Military Gain or Lose from Statehood?

Biggest Wins:
* Massive increase in military funding and technology.
* Stronger Arctic defense and more security.
* More jobs in the defense industry.

Biggest Risks:
* Losing independent military decision-making.
* Getting pulled into U.S. foreign conflicts.
* Possibly hosting U.S. nuclear weapons.

Would Canadians trade their independent peacekeeping reputation for the benefits of U.S. military funding?

Or would they say, "We'll keep NORAD, but we're good on statehood, thanks"?

One thing's for sure: If Canada became a U.S. state, it wouldn't just be a merger of economies and politics—it would completely reshape the future of North American defense.

| 11 |

Legal Frameworks

Would Canada even be legally allowed to join the U.S.?

Key Topics:
- The U.S. Constitution's rules for new states
- Would Canada need a national referendum?
- Could individual provinces join instead of the whole country?

Fun Fact: Texas is the only U.S. state that legally retained the right to split into five states. Could Canada do something similar?

The Law Says What?!

Could Canada Actually Join the U.S., or Is This Just a Fun Thought Experiment?

If there's one thing standing between Canada and U.S. statehood, it's not just public opinion, maple syrup diplomacy, or healthcare debates—it's the law.

Because as much as we love imagining a world where Mounties patrol alongside the NYPD, and Congress debates whether Tim Hortons should replace Starbucks, the real question is:

Could Canada legally become a U.S. state?

- Would the U.S. Constitution even allow it?
- Would Canada need a national referendum?
- Could individual provinces join instead of the whole country?

Let's dig into the legal roadblocks, loopholes, and constitutional quirks that could either make this the most epic geopolitical merger in history or a lawyer's nightmare.

1. Does the U.S. Constitution Allow This?

The Rules for Admitting New States
The U.S. Constitution actually has a process for admitting new states!

Article IV, Section 3 says:
"New States may be admitted by the Congress into this Union; but no new State shall be formed or erected within the jurisdiction of any other State... without the Consent of the Legislatures of the States concerned as well as of the Congress."

What Does That Mean for Canada?
* Congress has the power to admit new states.
* There's no rule against admitting an entire country as a state.
* Technically, Canada could apply for statehood if both countries agreed.

But there's a catch: The U.S. has never absorbed a fully independent country before.

- When the U.S. took in Hawaii, Texas, and Alaska, they were territories first—not full-fledged nations.

- The closest precedent is Texas, which was an independent country for about a decade before joining the U.S. in 1845.

Fun Fact: Texas is the only U.S. state that legally retained the right to split into five states if it ever wanted to. Could Canada negotiate something similar?

2. Would Canada Need a National Referendum?

Could Canada's Prime Minister Just Sign a Deal?
Nope. Not even close. Canada isn't a dictatorship (unless the raccoons take over Ottawa).

Canada's Constitution Act of 1982 protects its sovereignty, and any major changes require a national referendum or constitutional amendment.

Step 1: The Canadian Parliament would have to approve a bill proposing statehood.
Step 2: The proposal would likely trigger a national referendum (a country-wide vote).
Step 3: The U.S. Congress would need to accept Canada's application for statehood.

Translation: If Canada ever decided to join the U.S., it would need a nationwide debate, years of negotiations, and a public vote before anything happened.

Would Canadians Even Vote Yes?
Let's look at the biggest political obstacles to a YES vote:
* Loss of national identity – Canadians aren't just Americans with extra snow.
* Healthcare fears – Imagine a campaign ad saying "Vote YES and say goodbye to free healthcare!"

* Quebec's reaction – Quebec barely wants to stay in Canada as it is—would it ever join the U.S.? (Spoiler: Non.)

* U.S. politics – Would Canadians want to jump into the middle of U.S. partisan chaos?

Historical Note: In 1949, Newfoundland & Labrador held a referendum to decide whether to join Canada or remain independent. It was shockingly close—52% voted to join, 48% wanted independence.

Could a U.S.-Canada statehood vote be just as divisive?

3. Could Individual Provinces Join the U.S. Instead?

What if Canada didn't join as one state, but instead, some provinces applied for statehood separately?

This could actually be more legally feasible than merging the entire country.

- Article IV, Section 3 of the U.S. Constitution allows new states to be formed from existing land (as long as Congress approves).
- If a Canadian province held its own referendum and voted to apply for U.S. statehood, Congress could vote to accept it.
- This wouldn't require ALL of Canada to agree—just the provinces that want in.

Which Provinces Would Be Most Likely to Join?

Alberta & Saskatchewan – These provinces are politically more conservative and have strong economic ties to the U.S. (Also, Albertans sometimes joke about being the Texas of Canada.)

British Columbia – Already deeply connected to the U.S. West Coast economy, and Vancouver is basically Seattle but with better sushi.

Atlantic Provinces (Newfoundland, Nova Scotia, New Brunswick, PEI) – They have strong historical connections to the U.S. and some economic incentives to join.

Least Likely to Join? Quebec. (They'd probably declare independence first.)

Historical Example: Some in Alberta have floated the idea of separating from Canada over federal energy policies. If Alberta ever did secede, could it then apply for U.S. statehood?

4. Would Canada Need to Change Its Laws to Join the U.S.?

Canada's legal system is based on British common law, while the U.S. Constitution is... well, its own thing.

Biggest Legal Challenges:
- Canada has a parliamentary system. Would it switch to a governor and state legislature?
- Gun laws – Canada has stricter regulations; would those disappear? (Americans: "Come and take it." Canadians: "No thanks, we're good.")
- Language laws – Quebec has official language protections. Would those survive?
- Legal drinking age – Many Canadian provinces allow drinking at 18 or 19—would that change to 21? (Expect riots in Montreal.)

Basically, becoming a U.S. state wouldn't just be a political change—it would require massive legal restructuring.

5. Could the U.S. Force Canada to Join?

Short answer: Absolutely not.

The U.S. can't annex Canada (despite what conspiracy theorists say). Any merger would have to be entirely voluntary under international law.

Fun Fact: The U.S. tried to take Canada twice—once in the Revolutionary War and again in the War of 1812. It didn't go well.

So, no—statehood would have to be Canada's decision, not America's.

Final Thoughts: Could Canada Join the U.S. Under the Law?

Biggest Legal Obstacles:
* Canada would need a national referendum.
* Quebec and other provinces might refuse to join.
* Major legal restructuring would be required.

Biggest Legal Loopholes:
* The U.S. Constitution allows for new states to join.
* Individual provinces could theoretically apply for statehood separately.
* There's historical precedent (Texas, Hawaii) for independent entities joining the U.S.

Verdict?
It's legally possible, but extremely complicated. Any attempt at statehood would take decades, multiple legal battles, and a whole lot of political drama.

So while the law technically allows it, don't expect Canada to be on the U.S. flag anytime soon—unless, of course, Americans start offering free healthcare.

| 12 |

Constitutional Challenges

I f Canada were to join the United States, it wouldn't be as simple as just signing a treaty. It would require major constitutional changes—both in Canada and in the U.S.

This chapter explores the legal hurdles and the steps required to make statehood a reality.

Main Points & Objectives:
- Does the U.S. Constitution Allow This?
- Article IV, Section 3 of the U.S. Constitution states that Congress can admit new states.
- However, it has never dealt with absorbing an entire country before!
- Would Canada be treated like a territory seeking statehood (like Puerto Rico)?
- Would Canada Need a Constitutional Amendment?
- Canada's Constitution Act (1982) protects its sovereignty—statehood would likely require a national referendum or a major constitutional rewrite.
- Would all provinces need to agree, or could some join independently?
- Would the U.S. Need to Change its Structure?

- The balance of power in the Senate and Electoral College would shift.

- Would new constitutional amendments be required to accommodate a state as large as Canada?

- Legal Precedents: Has Anything Like This Happened Before?

- Texas was once an independent country before becoming a U.S. state.

- The U.S. has also annexed territories like Hawaii—but Canada's situation is different.

- Would the U.S. create a special status for Canada, or would it have to become individual states?

Fun Fact: The U.S. tried to annex Canada before—during the American Revolution and the War of 1812! Both times, Canadians said, "No thanks, eh!"

How Do You Merge Two Countries Without Breaking the Law (or Breaking Up Friendships)?

So... What's the Legal Fine Print on This Whole "Canada Becomes a U.S. State" Thing?

If Canada and the U.S. were just two friends on a road trip, merging might be as simple as flipping a coin, splitting gas money, and agreeing to play each other's Spotify playlists (yes, including Céline Dion and Bruce Springsteen).

But in reality, merging two entire nations is a legal nightmare.

- Would Canada need to rewrite its Constitution?

- Would the U.S. have to change its structure to accommodate a country this big?

- Could this even be done under existing laws, or would we need a legal magic wand?

Let's break down the constitutional roadblocks, potential loopholes, and historical precedents to see if statehood could actually happen—without making every lawyer in both countries cry.

1. Does the U.S. Constitution Allow This?

Yes, But It's Complicated.

The U.S. Constitution actually allows new states to be added—but it never anticipated absorbing an entire sovereign nation.

Article IV, Section 3 of the U.S. Constitution states:

"New States may be admitted by the Congress into this Union; but no new State shall be formed or erected within the jurisdiction of any other State... without the Consent of the Legislatures of the States concerned as well as of the Congress."

Translation? Congress CAN admit new states. But...
- It's never dealt with absorbing an entire foreign country before.
- The process has only applied to territories, not full-fledged independent nations.
- It's unclear how Canada's provinces would be treated—would they enter as one big state or multiple states?

Biggest Issue: The U.S. Constitution was written assuming new states would be territories first (like Hawaii, Alaska, and the western territories). Canada, however, is a fully developed, sovereign nation with its own government, laws, and maple syrup industry.

Could the U.S. just admit it as a state tomorrow? Legally... yes. Politically and logistically... not so fast.

2. Would Canada Need a Constitutional Amendment?

The Canadian Constitution Says, "Not So Fast, Buddy."

Unlike the U.S., which has a fairly flexible Constitution (and by "flexible," we mean it can be amended if everyone argues about it long enough), Canada's Constitution explicitly protects its sovereignty.

The Constitution Act of 1982 guarantees Canada's independence, meaning:

* Canada can't just be "absorbed" without a national vote.

* A major constitutional amendment would be required.

* All provinces would likely have to agree—cue instant Quebec drama.

Would Canada Need a Referendum?

Yes. If Canada wanted to join the U.S., it would almost certainly require a nationwide referendum, where every Canadian gets to vote on it.

Obstacles to a YES Vote:

- Quebec would almost certainly vote no (they already threaten to leave Canada every few decades).

- Some provinces, like British Columbia, have strong independent identities.

- Would Canadians want to switch from a parliamentary system to a presidential system?

Even if a referendum passed, Canada would have to rewrite major sections of its Constitution—a process that could take years, if not decades.

3. Would the U.S. Need to Change Its Structure?

Let's say Canada votes YES, and the U.S. is on board. The next question is:

How do you fit Canada into the U.S. political system without completely breaking it?

Biggest Issues:

1. The Senate: Right now, every U.S. state gets two Senators—would Canada only get two? Or would it be split into multiple states with 20+ Senators? (This would change U.S. politics forever.)

2. The Electoral College: Canada's 39 million people would mean dozens of new Electoral College votes, reshaping presidential elections.

3. The Balance of Power: Would Canada lean Democratic, Republican, or become a new swing region? (Expect politicians to start campaigning in Toronto real fast.)

Fun Fact: If Canada joined as a single state, it would instantly become the second-largest U.S. state by population, behind only California.

Would Americans be okay with giving that much power to Canada?

4. Legal Precedents: Has Anything Like This Happened Before?

The Texas Example

The closest example of a sovereign nation becoming a U.S. state is Texas.

- Texas was its own independent country from 1836 to 1845 before deciding to join the U.S.

- It negotiated special terms, including the right to split into five states if it wanted to.

- Could Canada negotiate similar terms? ("We'll join, but only if we keep free healthcare, bilingual road signs, and a national moose reserve.")

The Hawaii Example
- Hawaii was a kingdom, then a U.S. territory, then a state.
- It joined by popular vote—but its smaller population made the process easier.
- Canada's situation is way more complex since it's already a massive country.

Could the U.S. Create a "Special Status" for Canada?
- What if Canada became a state but retained more autonomy?
- Could it operate like Puerto Rico, with local self-governance but U.S. representation?
- Would Canada accept partial statehood or demand full rights?

5. Would All Provinces Have to Agree?

Tricky Question:
- Could Alberta join the U.S. while Quebec stays in Canada?
- Could individual provinces hold their own referendums?
- Would the U.S. allow "partial Canada statehood," or would it be all or nothing?

Historical Example: Some parts of Canada have debated closer ties with the U.S. before—especially Alberta, which has suggested greater economic integration.

But could one province leave Canada without the whole country going along? That's an entirely separate constitutional fight.

Final Thoughts: Could Statehood Legally Happen?

Biggest Legal Hurdles:
* Canada's Constitution would need major changes.
* A national referendum would likely be required.

* The U.S. would have to restructure Congress, the Senate, and the Electoral College.

Possible Loopholes:
* The U.S. Constitution does allow for new states—technically, Canada could apply.
* Canada could negotiate "special status" instead of full statehood.
* Individual provinces might be able to apply separately.

Would it be legally possible? Technically, yes.
Would it be politically and logistically insane? Also yes.

Bottom line: Canada joining the U.S. would require more legal paperwork than a law school final exam—and enough political drama to make reality TV look tame.

Fun Fact: The U.S. Has Already Tried to Annex Canada—Twice!
- The American Revolution (1775-1783): The U.S. tried to convince Canada to join. Canada politely declined.
- The War of 1812: The U.S. actually invaded Canada, thinking it would be an easy win. Spoiler: It was not.

So if Canada ever voluntarily joined, it would be a historical first—after two failed attempts by force.

| 13 |

Indigenous Rights and Treaties

C anada has a unique legal framework for Indigenous rights, including land treaties and self-governance agreements. If Canada joined the U.S., would these rights still be protected, or would Indigenous nations face the same challenges as Native American tribes under U.S. law?

Main Points & Objectives:
- How Canada Treats Indigenous Sovereignty
- Indigenous nations in Canada have constitutional protections under Section 35 of the Constitution Act.
- The Indian Act (while controversial) establishes special legal status and land rights.
- Canada has been working toward reconciliation, recognizing Indigenous self-governance.
- How the U.S. Treats Native American Tribes
- In the U.S., Native American tribes are treated as "domestic dependent nations."
- Tribal sovereignty exists, but the U.S. government has historically violated treaties and forced assimilation policies.
- Would Canadian First Nations want to risk losing their current legal status?
- Would Canadian Indigenous Groups Accept U.S. Jurisdiction?

- Many Indigenous leaders in Canada oppose closer ties with the U.S. due to the historical treatment of Native Americans.
- Would First Nations groups demand a special status in the U.S.?
- Could they negotiate a unique arrangement that allows greater sovereignty?
- What Happens to Existing Land Treaties?
- The U.S. has often broken Indigenous treaties—would Canada's be honored?
- Would land claims and resource-sharing agreements be renegotiated?
- How would U.S. corporations affect Indigenous land rights in resource-rich provinces?

Fun Fact: Canada has a larger percentage of Indigenous population than the U.S., and many First Nations communities already span the U.S.-Canada border—like the Mohawk Nation of Akwesasne, which exists in both countries!

Would Canada's First Nations Gain, Lose, or Demand Their Own Deal?

The Question No One Can Ignore: What About Indigenous Sovereignty?

If Canada became a U.S. state (or multiple states), it wouldn't just be about trade agreements, healthcare debates, or a new star on the American flag—it would also mean a huge shift in Indigenous governance, land rights, and treaties.

And let's be real: Indigenous nations have heard this story before.

- Promises of respect? *
- Agreements to protect land rights? *
- Governments eventually breaking those agreements? Also *.

So if Canada joined the U.S., would First Nations, Métis, and Inuit peoples see their rights respected, or would they face the same legal and historical challenges as Native American tribes in the U.S.?

Let's break down how Indigenous governance works in Canada vs. the U.S., and whether this would be a dealbreaker for Canadian statehood.

1. How Canada Treats Indigenous Sovereignty

Indigenous rights in Canada are constitutionally recognized, meaning:

The Canadian Constitution Act (1982) – Section 35
- Recognizes and affirms Indigenous rights, land claims, and self-governance.
- Guarantees that future laws must respect Indigenous treaties.
- Gives Indigenous nations legal leverage when negotiating with the government.

The Indian Act (1876, still in effect today)
- Establishes special legal status for Indigenous peoples.
- Defines the reserve system (where Indigenous land is legally protected).
- Has a complicated history (many Indigenous communities want to reform or replace it).

Translation: In Canada, Indigenous nations have stronger legal protections than in the U.S.. While there's still a long way to go in reconciliation, Canada has been moving toward:
* More self-governance agreements.
* Financial settlements for past land claims.
* Recognition of Indigenous law alongside Canadian law.

So... what happens if those protections suddenly fall under U.S. jurisdiction?

2. How the U.S. Treats Native American Tribes

Now, let's compare this to how Indigenous sovereignty works in the United States.

The U.S. recognizes Native American tribes as "domestic dependent nations."
- This means tribes are sovereign, but also subject to U.S. federal law.
- Tribal governments can pass laws, but Congress can override them.

Treaty History in the U.S.? Not Great.
- Many treaties signed between Indigenous nations and the U.S. were eventually broken.
- The U.S. has a history of forced assimilation policies (such as boarding schools and the Dawes Act, which divided tribal land).
- While modern tribal sovereignty has improved, legal battles over land, resources, and jurisdiction still happen constantly.

Big Question: Would Canada's Indigenous groups risk losing their stronger legal standing to enter a system that has historically been less protective?

(Short answer: Probably not willingly.)

3. Would Canadian Indigenous Groups Accept U.S. Jurisdiction?

This might be the biggest dealbreaker in the entire Canada-U.S. statehood debate.

First Nations groups in Canada have already said they do not want U.S. influence.

Many Indigenous leaders in Canada view U.S. Indigenous policy as weaker and less protective of rights.

Would Indigenous nations demand a special legal status in the U.S., separate from Native American tribes?

Possible Scenarios If Canada Joined the U.S.:

1. Indigenous Nations Reject Statehood Entirely
- Indigenous communities could refuse to participate in the statehood process.
- Some First Nations might even push for independent nation status, rather than being part of Canada or the U.S. (This would get legally complicated, fast.)

2. Indigenous Nations Negotiate a Special Agreement
- Could Canadian Indigenous groups demand a unique arrangement, keeping their current constitutional protections even under U.S. rule?
- Would they push for even more autonomy, such as their own territory separate from U.S. statehood?

Indigenous Rights Get Merged into U.S. Policy (Not Ideal for Them)
- If the U.S. forced Canadian First Nations to follow U.S. tribal law, they would lose constitutional protections they currently enjoy.
- Land rights could become vulnerable to U.S. government decisions (not a great history there).
- Indigenous leaders would likely resist this, legally and politically.

Fun Fact: Many Indigenous nations already span the U.S.-Canada border. The Mohawk Nation of Akwesasne, for example, has communities in New York, Ontario, and Quebec.

Would those cross-border nations suddenly have to follow different legal systems?

4. What Happens to Existing Land Treaties?

Biggest legal question: Would Canada's Indigenous land treaties still be honored under U.S. law?

In Canada, First Nations negotiate directly with the government for land rights, financial compensation, and self-governance.

In the U.S., Native American tribes often have to fight in court for land and resource rights—sometimes losing those battles to corporations or federal agencies.

Potential Problems with Merging Treaty Systems:
* Would the U.S. recognize Canadian land treaties, or would they demand renegotiation?
* Could corporations push for oil, mining, or pipeline projects on Indigenous land?
* Would U.S. courts interfere in land disputes that were already settled under Canadian law?

Historical Warning: The U.S. has a long history of disregarding Indigenous land claims when resources (oil, gas, minerals) are involved. If Canada's Indigenous groups suddenly lost their legal protections... well, history suggests it wouldn't end well for them.

5. Could Indigenous Nations Choose a Different Path?

If Canada joined the U.S., could its Indigenous nations choose to remain independent instead?

Some Indigenous groups could seek full sovereignty, outside both Canada and the U.S.

Could the U.S. create a new category for Canadian First Nations, recognizing them as sovereign nations with unique rights?

Or would this just become another century-long legal battle?

Would Canada's First Nations demand a seat at the negotiating table—before Canada even considers statehood? (Most likely, yes.)

Final Thoughts: Indigenous Sovereignty as a Dealbreaker?

Biggest Risks for Indigenous Groups:
* Losing stronger legal protections under Canadian law.
* Being forced into the U.S. tribal system, which has a weaker track record.
* Having to fight new legal battles over land and resources.

Possible Loopholes or Solutions:
* Demanding a unique legal status within the U.S.
* Negotiating a higher level of sovereignty than U.S. tribes currently have.
* Refusing to participate in statehood altogether—possibly pushing for full independence.

Would Canadian First Nations accept U.S. statehood? Probably not without massive concessions. And if they reject it, could Canada even move forward with statehood at all?

This could be one of the biggest obstacles in the entire debate.

Bottom Line: If Canada ever seriously considered joining the U.S., expect Indigenous nations to demand a MAJOR role in negotiations—or reject the entire idea outright.

| 14 |

The U.S. Political Divide

The U.S. parties would have very different reactions.

Key Topics:
- Republican views: Pro-business, but concerned about "big government" expansion
- Democratic views: Pro-social programs, but nervous about new conservative regions
- Dad Joke: Why do politicians always bring a pencil to the party? Because they want to draw votes!

Would Canada Be a Blue State, a Red State... or Just Really Confused?

Would America's Two-Party System Survive the Great Canadian Invasion?

If Canada became a U.S. state (or multiple states), it wouldn't just change Canada—it would fundamentally alter the entire American political landscape.

Now, Americans love a good political debate almost as much as they love arguing about who makes the best barbecue. But if you throw 39 million Canadians into the mix, the U.S. might need a whole new playbook.

- Would Canada be a solidly Democratic region?
- Would conservative provinces like Alberta boost Republican power?
- Would American political parties change their platforms to attract new Canadian voters?

Let's break down how Republicans and Democrats would react to Canada joining the U.S.—and why this might be the biggest political shake-up since America started calling French fries "freedom fries."

1. The Republican View: Pro-Business, But Skeptical of Big Government Expansion

What Republicans Would Like About Canadian Statehood

Big Business Wins – More U.S. states mean more investment opportunities, fewer trade barriers, and a bigger North American economic zone.

Energy & Oil Expansion – Alberta and Saskatchewan are major oil-producing regions. Republicans—especially those from Texas and Oklahoma—would love boosting U.S. energy independence by fully integrating Canada's oil industry.

Stronger Border Security? – Some Republicans might see absorbing Canada as a way to eliminate illegal border crossings. (Even though, let's be real—no one is illegally sneaking into the U.S. from Canada unless they REALLY love Florida weather.)

What Republicans Would Hate About Canadian Statehood

Big Government Expansion – The GOP already argues that the federal government is too big. Adding a massive new state (or several) with different laws would be seen as another layer of bureaucracy.

Canada's Love of Socialism – Republicans tend to oppose so-cialized healthcare, environmental regulations, and high taxes—a.k.a. Canada's entire personality. They might resist statehood for fear of turning America into an even more liberal country.

Canadian Culture Shock – How would Republican strongholds like Alabama or Kentucky react to millions of polite, hockey-loving, healthcare-defending voters entering the system? Probably with some well-placed side-eye.

Biggest Fear: If Canada joins, it could permanently tip the U.S. to-ward the Democrats. Which brings us to...

2. The Democratic View: More Social Programs, But Worried About New Conservative Voters

What Democrats Would Like About Canadian Statehood

Universal Healthcare Momentum – Millions of new voters from a country that already has universal healthcare? That's a dream come true for Democrats pushing for Medicare-for-All.

Stronger Climate Policies – Canada is more progressive on en-vironmental laws than the U.S., which means Democrats could gain more support for green energy policies.

More Blue States? – If Canada became one giant state, it would have enough population to tilt presidential elections toward Democ-rats permanently. (Bye-bye, swing states!)

What Democrats Would Hate About Canadian Statehood

Rural Conservative Provinces – Alberta and Saskatchewan are more like Texas than California—big on oil, low taxes, and not huge fans of government intervention.

Electoral College Drama – If each Canadian province became its own state, suddenly conservative provinces could balance out traditionally liberal ones.

Shift in Political Priorities – Right now, the U.S. political debate is heavily focused on issues like healthcare, gun control, and taxes. If Canada joins, suddenly issues like Indigenous rights, Arctic defense, and bilingual policies become central. Would Democrats be ready for that shift?

Biggest Fear: What if Canada isn't as solidly liberal as Democrats assume? If the U.S. political divide already looks like a hockey fight, throwing 10 new states into the ring might create a political brawl no one can predict.

3. Could Canada Create a Third Major Political Force?

Right now, the U.S. political system is a two-party battle between Democrats and Republicans. But in Canada, there are multiple political parties, including:

Liberal Party (Canada's "Democrats")
Conservative Party (Canada's "Republicans")
New Democratic Party (More progressive than U.S. Democrats)
Bloc Québécois (Would probably just quit politics entirely if Canada joined the U.S.)
Green Party (Would absolutely love to see the U.S. adopt Canada's climate policies)

Could Canada introduce a viable third party into U.S. politics?

- If Canada's political factions didn't fully align with U.S. Democrats or Republicans, could they form a new centrist or left-wing movement?
- Could Canadian voters push America toward a multi-party system like in Europe?
- Would moderate voters flee to a new "Canadian-style" political party?

This could be the biggest unintended consequence of Canadian statehood—breaking the two-party system once and for all.

4. The Electoral College Earthquake

Right now, the U.S. Electoral College is designed for 50 states.

If Canada joined as one state, it would have about 50-55 electoral votes—more than Florida and New York, making it a political powerhouse.

If each province became a separate state:
* Ontario would have more electoral votes than Illinois.
* Quebec would be a swing state with huge influence.
* Alberta and Saskatchewan could boost Republican chances.

Would this create a permanent Democratic majority, or would conservative provinces balance things out?

Final Thoughts: Would Either Party Support Canadian Statehood?

Biggest Wins for Republicans:

* More economic growth, oil industry expansion.
* More conservative voters from rural Canada.
* Stronger border security.

Biggest Wins for Democrats:
* More support for universal healthcare and climate policies.
* Liberal-leaning provinces could tilt elections permanently blue.
* Could push the U.S. toward a multi-party system.

Biggest Risks for Both Parties:
* The political balance could shift in unpredictable ways.
* The Electoral College could become unmanageable.
* A third-party movement could disrupt both Democrats and Republicans.

So, would the U.S. political system survive the "Canadian Takeover"?

Or would it be the political equivalent of a game of hockey with no referees?

One thing is clear: If Canada ever joined the U.S., it wouldn't just be a bigger country—it would be a different country.

| 15 |

Canada's Political Divide

Canada is not politically uniform—each province has its own priorities, ideologies, and cultural identity. Some regions are more open to U.S. influence than others. This chapter explores how different provinces might react to U.S. statehood.

Main Points & Objectives:
- Western Provinces (Alberta, Saskatchewan, Manitoba)
  - Historically more conservative and resource-based economies
  - Many Albertans have supported stronger U.S. economic ties (even separatist movements)
  - Could these provinces opt to join separately from the rest of Canada?
- Quebec's Dilemma
  - Strong separatist history—would they rather be independent than join the U.S.?
  - French-language preservation concerns
- Ontario and British Columbia: The Political Middle Ground
  - Economic powerhouses, politically mixed
  - More likely to resist change due to economic stability
- Atlantic Canada: A Different Perspective
  - Close economic ties to the U.S. but culturally distinct
  - Would rural communities accept the shift?

Fun Fact: During a 2004 political scandal, a movement called "The Republic of Alberta" briefly gained traction as some Albertans joked about becoming the 51st U.S. state!

Would Canada Join the U.S. as One... or Would It Be a Political Family Feud?

Would Canada Actually Agree to This... or Would It Fall Apart Before the Deal Even Starts?

Let's face it—Canada is not one big, unified political block. It's a mosaic of provinces, each with its own culture, economy, and strong opinions on everything from taxes to hockey teams.

So, if Canada ever seriously considered joining the U.S., would the entire country be on board?

Spoiler alert: Probably not.

Some provinces might enthusiastically sign up, others would hesitate, and Quebec... well, Quebec might just drop the mic and walk away.

Let's break down how different regions of Canada would react to statehood and whether this would be a smooth transition—or a political breakup waiting to happen.

1. Western Provinces (Alberta, Saskatchewan, Manitoba) – The Conservative, Pro-Business Side of Canada

Would Alberta & Saskatchewan Say "Yeehaw, Let's Do It"?

If there's one part of Canada that might actually consider U.S. statehood, it's Alberta and Saskatchewan.

Oil & Energy Politics – Alberta and Saskatchewan have huge oil reserves and often clash with Ottawa over energy regulations. They might prefer U.S. energy policies, which tend to favor fewer restrictions and more development.

Political Leanings – These provinces lean conservative, more in line with U.S. Republican policies.

Separatist Movements Already Exist – Alberta has had pro-secession movements in the past (like the "Republic of Alberta" movement in 2004), arguing that the province would be better off outside of Canada's federal system.

Would Manitoba Join the U.S. or Stay Canadian?

Manitoba is a wild card. It's politically mixed, with conservative rural areas and a progressive urban center (Winnipeg).

- Would it follow Alberta and Saskatchewan into statehood?
- Or would it stick with Ontario and the rest of Canada?

Big Question: If Alberta and Saskatchewan wanted to leave Canada and join the U.S., would Canada even let them go?

(That's an entirely different constitutional fight!)

2. Quebec – Would It Rather Go Solo?

If Canada were a reality TV show, Quebec would be the dramatic contestant who threatens to quit every season.

Would Quebec Join the U.S.? Probably Not.

Quebec is the most politically and culturally distinct province in Canada.

Major Issues Quebec Would Have With U.S. Statehood:
French Language Rights – Quebec has strong protections for the French language. Would the U.S. guarantee that? (Doubtful.)

Separatist History – Quebec has held two referendums (1980 & 1995) on leaving Canada. If they don't even like being part of Canada, why would they join the U.S.?

Economic & Social Differences – Quebec has progressive policies on healthcare, social services, and government intervention. It's unlikely they'd want to be absorbed into the U.S.'s more privatized system.

Would Quebec Declare Independence Instead?

It's possible! Instead of joining the U.S. or staying in Canada, Quebec could say:

"You know what? We're out. We're just gonna be our own country now."

Big Question: If Canada fractured because of statehood debates, could Quebec actually use this as an opportunity to finally declare independence?

3. Ontario & British Columbia – The Political Middle Ground

Ontario and British Columbia are Canada's two economic powerhouses—so what would they think about statehood?

Ontario – Too Big to Take a Risk?

Ontario is Canada's most populous province, with over 14.5 million people—almost as many as New York State.

Why Ontario Might Oppose Statehood:
- It has the strongest ties to Canada's existing system—why mess with that?
- It's politically mixed, meaning it wouldn't benefit as much from a shift to U.S. governance.
- Toronto's economy is already globally competitive—would it gain much from becoming "just another U.S. city"?

Big Question: Would Ontario lose power in a bigger, U.S.-led system? Right now, it's Canada's center of power. In the U.S., it would be just another state.

British Columbia – Culturally U.S.-Friendly, But Would It Say Yes?

West Coast Identity – Culturally, B.C. feels more connected to Seattle and California than to Ottawa.

Economic Strength – Vancouver is a major economic hub—it might actually benefit from closer ties to U.S. tech and trade.
Progressive Politics – B.C. is more in line with West Coast liberal values, which could make U.S. statehood less of a cultural shock.

Would British Columbia consider breaking away from Canada and joining as an independent West Coast U.S. state? Maybe—but it's still a long shot.

4. Atlantic Canada – Closer to the U.S., But Would It Want to Join?

Economically Tied to the U.S. – Atlantic Canada (Newfoundland, Nova Scotia, New Brunswick, and PEI) has strong trade connections to the U.S.

Fishing Industry – These provinces rely heavily on seafood exports to the U.S., which means joining the U.S. could benefit their economy.

Cultural Distinctiveness – These provinces have a strong regional identity—would they be willing to give up their Canadian heritage?

Big Question: Would Atlantic Canada feel like they were too small to have influence in the U.S. political system?

5. Could Provinces Choose Their Own Path?

Biggest Legal Question: Does all of Canada have to join together, or could provinces join separately?

Some possible scenarios:
* All of Canada joins as one big state. (Unlikely—too many regional differences.)
* Each province becomes its own state. (Would the U.S. really want 10+ new states overnight?)
* Some provinces join, while others stay in Canada. (This would get legally messy FAST.)

Fun Fact: The U.S. Constitution does not require a country to join all at once—so individual provinces could theoretically apply separately!

Final Thoughts: Would Canada Even Stay Together During This Debate?

Most Likely To Consider Joining the U.S.:

* Alberta & Saskatchewan (More conservative, resource-based economies)

* British Columbia (Culturally West Coast, economically tied to the U.S.)

Most Likely To Oppose Statehood:

* Quebec (Would rather be its own country than join the U.S.)

* Ontario (Too big to risk losing its status in Canada)

Wild Card Regions:

Atlantic Canada (Might consider it for economic reasons, but culturally hesitant)

Manitoba (Politically mixed—depends on the other provinces' decisions)

Bottom Line: The "Canada joins the U.S." debate could actually lead to Canada breaking apart. Instead of one new U.S. state, we might end up with:

- A few Canadian provinces joining the U.S.
- Quebec going independent
- Ontario and the Atlantic provinces staying Canadian

Would that be a new era of North American unity—or the messiest divorce in political history?

| 16 |

Education Systems

Would Canada's education system fit within the U.S. model? With differences in funding, curriculum, and even school culture, this chapter examines the practical and philosophical challenges of merging the two systems.

Main Points & Objectives:
- Funding Differences
  - U.S.: State-based, varying quality, heavy reliance on property taxes
  - Canada: Federally standardized, stronger public funding
- Curriculum & Testing
  - U.S.: Common Core, AP exams, state-specific standards
  - Canada: Provincial autonomy in curriculum, nationalized approach to literacy/math
- Higher Education & Student Debt
  - U.S.: Expensive tuition, reliance on student loans
  - Canada: Heavily subsidized public universities
  - Would Canadian students suddenly be saddled with U.S.-level debt?
- School Culture: Hockey vs. Football
  - U.S.: High school football dominates, pep rallies, homecoming culture
  - Canada: Hockey is king, education more academic-focused

Fun Fact: If Canada joined the U.S., Harvard and Yale would gain thousands of top-tier hockey recruits overnight!

Would Canadian Schools Get an American Makeover, or Would the U.S. Start Learning in Metric?

Would Canada's Education System Survive the U.S. School System... or Would It Be Sent to Detention?

When you merge two countries, you don't just combine economies, military forces, and healthcare policies—you also have to figure out what kids are going to learn, how schools will be funded, and whether students will end up drowning in student loans.

The U.S. and Canada have very different approaches to education, from funding models to curriculum to what counts as an acceptable excuse for missing school ("snowstorm" is a perfectly valid reason in Canada).

So, if Canada became a U.S. state (or multiple states), how would the education system adapt?
- Would Canadian schools have to follow U.S. standards like Common Core?
- Would tuition skyrocket for Canadian college students?
- Would Canada introduce mandatory hockey classes to U.S. schools? (Okay, maybe that one's a stretch—but admit it, it would be fun.)

Let's break down the practical, financial, and cultural clashes of merging these two education systems.

1. Funding Differences – Who Pays for Schools?

How Schools Are Funded in the U.S.

Public schools in the U.S. are primarily funded by property taxes.

Wealthier neighborhoods = better-funded schools with newer textbooks, better facilities, and more programs.

Poorer neighborhoods = underfunded schools, outdated supplies, and fewer extracurricular activities.

Biggest Problem? Since education funding depends on local taxes, there is a huge gap between wealthy and low-income school districts.

How Schools Are Funded in Canada

* Education is publicly funded across all provinces, with federal oversight.

* The quality of schools doesn't vary as much by location because funding is more evenly distributed.

* The system ensures more equal access to resources, regardless of wealth.

Would Canada's More Equitable System Survive in the U.S.?

If Canada joined the U.S., would it:

1. Adopt the American system—where school quality depends on local taxes?

2. Keep its national funding model—which could pressure the U.S. to reconsider its own approach?

3. Create a hybrid system—where Canadian states fund schools differently from the rest of the U.S.?

This could be one of the biggest fights in a potential merger. Would American parents push for the Canadian model once they see it? Or would Canada be forced into the American system—leading to declining school quality in some provinces?

2. Curriculum & Testing – Would Canada Have to Adopt Common Core?

How Curriculum Works in the U.S.

- Education is controlled at the state level, leading to 50 different versions of what kids learn.

- Some states emphasize STEM, while others focus more on standardized testing.

- Common Core standards attempt to create national consistency (but not all states follow them).

- High school students take AP exams, SATs, and ACTs to get into college.

Biggest Issue? A student in Massachusetts might get a world-class education, while a student in Mississippi might be learning from 20-year-old textbooks.

How Curriculum Works in Canada

* Each province sets its own curriculum, but with more national consistency.

* More emphasis on literacy, math, and science than on standardized testing.

* No SATs or ACTs—university admissions are based on high school performance.

* Less focus on "teaching to the test" compared to the U.S.

Would Canada Have to Switch to U.S.-Style Testing?

If Canada became a U.S. state:

- Would Canadian students suddenly have to take SATs, ACTs, and AP exams?

- Would provinces lose their curriculum control to Washington?

- Would Canadian schools adopt U.S. history lessons (goodbye, War of 1812, hello, Revolutionary War)?

Canadian students currently don't spend as much time prepping for standardized tests—would they lose that advantage under a U.S. education model?

3. Higher Education & Student Debt – Will Canadian Students Go Bankrupt?

The U.S. College System: Expensive, Stressful, and Full of Debt
- American universities are among the best in the world... but also the most expensive.
- Tuition at a top U.S. school can cost $50,000+ per year.
- Many students graduate with massive student debt—sometimes $100,000 or more.
- Community colleges exist as a cheaper option, but they lack prestige.

The Canadian University System: Affordable and Accessible
* Public universities are heavily subsidized, making tuition much cheaper.
* Tuition is typically between $5,000-$10,000 per year (compared to $50,000 in the U.S.).
* Less reliance on student loans—most students graduate without massive debt.
* University admissions are based on high school grades, no SATs required.

Biggest Concern? Would Canadian Students Suddenly Face U.S.-Style Tuition Costs?
If Canada became part of the U.S.:
- Would public university funding be cut—leading to higher tuition?
- Would Canadian students be forced into the U.S. student loan system?

- Would Canada's strong university reputation be affected by a switch in funding?

Or—would Canada convince Americans to adopt its lower-cost education model instead? (Imagine that—Americans thanking Canada for cheaper college tuition!)

4. School Culture – Hockey vs. Football, Pep Rallies vs. More Academics

Beyond curriculum and funding, school culture is very different in Canada and the U.S.

U.S. School Culture: Go Big or Go Home!
High School Football is a Religion – Friday night lights, cheerleaders, massive stadiums, and homecoming traditions.
Extracurriculars Rule – Marching bands, debate clubs, student government—there's an activity for everyone.
Prom and Pep Rallies Are a Big Deal – School spirit is a huge part of American education.

Canadian School Culture: More Academics, Less Spectacle
Hockey is King – While U.S. schools rally around football, Canadian schools prioritize hockey.
- More Academically Focused – Canadian schools have extracurriculars, but there's less pressure on school spirit compared to the U.S.
- More Focus on Getting Into University – Fewer pep rallies, more emphasis on grades and university admissions.

Would Canadian Schools Get the Full American High School Experience?
- Would high schools in Ontario and Quebec suddenly get massive football stadiums?

- Would Alberta and Manitoba see marching bands and home-coming dances take over?

- Or would Canada's more academic-focused schools influence U.S. education instead?

Final Thoughts: Would the Education Merger Be a Win or a Loss?

Biggest Wins for Canada:

* Access to top U.S. universities (Harvard, MIT, Stanford, etc.).

* More investment in research and innovation.

* More athletic scholarships for Canadian hockey players.

Biggest Risks for Canada:

* Risk of losing public education funding.

* Higher university tuition and student debt.

* More standardized testing, less curriculum independence.

Biggest Wins for the U.S.:

* Stronger public school funding model to study.

* More top-tier students entering American universities.

* Potential influence from Canada's lower-cost university model.

Biggest Risks for the U.S.:

* Would Americans push to adopt the Canadian funding model?

* Would elite U.S. universities have to change their admissions process?

* Would U.S. schools suddenly have to build hockey arenas? (Okay, maybe that's not a "risk.")

So—would Canadian schools get Americanized, or would the U.S. learn a few lessons from Canada?

| 17 |

Social Policies

W ould Canadians have to adjust to different tax structures and social benefits? This chapter compares Canada's social policies with those of the U.S., highlighting what might change.

Main Points & Objectives:
- Taxes & Government Spending
  - U.S.: Lower taxes overall, but fewer social services
  - Canada: Higher taxes, stronger social safety net
  - Would Canadians accept U.S.-style taxation?
- Social Security & Retirement Benefits
  - U.S.: Social Security is underfunded, individual responsibility for 401(k)s
  - Canada: Stronger public pension system, less reliance on employer benefits
- Unemployment Benefits & Workers' Rights
  - Canada: Generous leave policies, stronger worker protections
  - U.S.: More employer-based benefits, weaker union influence

Fun Fact: Canadians get more paid vacation than Americans. In Canada, employees receive at least two weeks of paid vacation by law, while in the U.S., there is no federal requirement for paid vacation. Canadians would not be happy about losing that perk!

Would Canadians Trade Their Social Safety Net for Lower Taxes... or Just Riot in the Streets?

Would Canadians Adjust to the U.S. Model... or Would Americans Start Demanding Canadian Benefits?

If Canada became part of the U.S., one of the biggest adjustments wouldn't be the flag, the healthcare system, or even driving on the right side of the road (wait, they already do that!)—it would be social policies.

For Canadians, government-funded social services like universal healthcare, paid parental leave, and strong retirement benefits are as much a part of life as hockey and apologizing for no reason.

For Americans, social policies operate on a very different model—lower taxes, but also fewer guaranteed government benefits.

So, if Canada joined the U.S.:
- Would Canadians accept lower taxes in exchange for fewer social services?
- Would Americans demand an upgrade to their benefits after seeing what Canada has?
- Would workers in Canada lose their stronger labor protections?

Let's break down how welfare, taxes, and retirement benefits differ between Canada and the U.S.—and what would happen if the two systems had to merge.

1. Taxes & Government Spending – Who Pays More, and Who Gets More?

If there's one thing Americans love, it's lower taxes. If there's one thing Canadians love, it's getting their money's worth from taxes.

Taxation: U.S. vs. Canada

U.S. Taxes:
- The U.S. has lower taxes overall, especially on income and sales taxes.
- Federal income tax rates range from 10% to 37%, depending on income.
- Sales tax varies by state but is typically lower than Canada's (though some states, like Oregon, have no sales tax at all).

Canadian Taxes:
- Canada has higher income taxes, with federal rates ranging from 15% to 33%—but provinces also add their own taxes, meaning total rates can go much higher.
- Sales tax (GST + provincial tax) is often over 13%, making everything from groceries to gas more expensive than in most U.S. states.
- Corporate taxes are higher, especially for large businesses.

Would Canadians Accept U.S.-Style Taxation?

If Canada became a U.S. state:
* Canadians would pay lower taxes overall.
* But they'd also lose many of their government-funded benefits.
* Would Canadians be willing to trade "free" healthcare for a bigger paycheck? (Survey says: Probably not.)

Would Americans Accept Higher Taxes for More Benefits?

If Canada kept its social programs under U.S. statehood, it could pressure Americans to ask:

- "Why do Canadians get free healthcare and better retirement benefits while we don't?"
- "Should the U.S. increase taxes to pay for better social services?"

Could Canada accidentally start a tax-and-welfare revolution in the U.S.?

2. Social Security & Retirement – Who Gets to Retire Happily?

Let's talk about retirement.

In Canada:
- The Canada Pension Plan (CPP) is publicly funded and mandatory—every worker pays into it and gets benefits when they retire.
- Old Age Security (OAS) is another federally funded program that provides retirement income for seniors.
- Canadians don't have to rely on employer-based retirement plans.

In the U.S.:
- Social Security is the American version of CPP, but it's underfunded and projected to run into financial trouble in the coming decades.
- Most Americans have to set up their own 401(k) retirement plans—which depend on stock market performance and employer contributions.
- If your employer doesn't offer a good retirement plan? Good luck retiring comfortably.

Would Canada's Pension System Survive U.S. Statehood?

- Would Canadians be forced into the U.S. system—meaning less reliable government retirement benefits?

- Would Canada's pension system influence U.S. reforms—making American retirement more secure?

Would U.S. Workers Demand a Canadian-Style Pension?

If Americans saw that Canada's retirement system was more reliable, would they start demanding a stronger Social Security system?

Would Canada improve retirement benefits for the U.S., or would the U.S. weaken retirement benefits for Canadians?

3. Unemployment Benefits & Workers' Rights – Would Canada Lose Its Worker Protections?

Let's say you lose your job. What happens next?

In Canada:
- Employment Insurance (EI) covers workers who lose their jobs, offering higher benefits for longer periods than U.S. unemployment.
- Parental leave is much better—up to 12-18 months of paid leave for new parents.
- Stronger union protections—making it harder for companies to fire workers unfairly.

In the U.S.:
- Unemployment benefits vary by state and are often lower and shorter-term than in Canada.
- Parental leave? What parental leave? There is no federally required paid parental leave in the U.S.—it depends on your employer.
- Weaker union protections—in many states, workers can be fired at will, meaning fewer job security guarantees.

Would Canadian Workers Be Okay With U.S. Labor Laws?

If Canada joined the U.S.:
* Parental leave benefits would likely shrink.
* Unemployment benefits could be reduced.
* Union protections might weaken.

Would Canadian workers protest for stronger protections? Would the U.S. labor movement gain momentum from newly added Canadian workers?

Or would Canada's workers just have to accept weaker benefits?

(Expect some major protests if that happened.)

4. Vacation Time – Would Canadians Lose Their Precious Days Off?

Fun Fact: The U.S. is one of the only developed countries in the world with no federally mandated paid vacation days.

In Canada:
- Workers are guaranteed at least two weeks of paid vacation per year—many jobs offer more.
- Some provinces require three weeks or more after a certain number of years working.

In the U.S.:
- There is no federal vacation policy. Employers aren't required to give paid vacation.
- Many jobs offer only 10 days per year—and some don't offer any!

Would Canadians Accept Losing Their Paid Time Off?

Imagine telling Canadians:

"Welcome to America! By the way, your vacation just got cut in half."

(Expect a national crisis.)

Final Thoughts: Would Canadians Accept U.S. Social Policies?

Biggest Wins for Canadians:
* Lower taxes overall.
* Access to a bigger job market.
* Stronger economic opportunities in some sectors.

Biggest Risks for Canadians:
* Losing universal healthcare.
* Losing strong labor laws and parental leave.
* Losing a reliable public pension system.
* Possibly paying more for education and retirement benefits.

Biggest Wins for Americans:
* Potential for better government retirement benefits.
* Possibility of learning from Canada's worker protections.
* Could increase pressure to reform social policies.

Biggest Risks for Americans:
* Would taxes need to go up to fund more benefits?
* Would businesses resist stronger labor protections?
* Would there be a culture clash over vacation time, paid leave, and social programs?

Would Canada's stronger social policies survive in the U.S., or would they disappear?

Would Canadians accept fewer benefits for lower taxes?

Or would Americans see Canada's model and say, "Hey, wait a minute... why don't we have that?"

| 18 |

Economic Impacts

Would merging the two economies be beneficial, or would it cause financial chaos? This chapter evaluates the financial feasibility of statehood, weighing the pros and cons.

Main Points & Objectives:
- U.S. Debt vs. Canadian Stability
  - The U.S. has over $34 trillion in debt—would Canada inherit some of it?
  - Canada's economy is stable but smaller—could it withstand U.S. economic turbulence?
- Impact on Key Industries
  - Oil & Gas (Alberta vs. U.S. regulations)
  - Banking & Financial Institutions (Canada's stricter financial regulations vs. U.S. free-market approach)
- Trade & Business Integration
  - Would NAFTA/USMCA even be necessary anymore?
  - Could businesses benefit from a single economic system?
- Would Canadians Lose or Gain Financially?
  - Would wages go up or down?
  - Would businesses relocate to the U.S. for tax benefits?

Fun Fact: If Canada became a U.S. state, its GDP would be larger than Texas but smaller than California—making it the second-most economically powerful state in America!

Would This Be the Biggest Economic Merger in History... or a Financial Disaster?

Would Canada and the U.S. Be Richer Together... or Just Create a Giant Economic Mess?

If Canada and the U.S. became one country, it wouldn't just be a political and cultural transformation—it would also be one of the biggest economic shifts in history.

Imagine merging:
- The world's largest economy (the U.S.) with one of the most stable economies (Canada).
- A low-tax, high-debt system (U.S.) with a high-tax, low-debt system (Canada).
- A free-market banking system (U.S.) with a tightly regulated banking system (Canada).

So, the big question is:
- Would this make North America an economic powerhouse... or a bureaucratic nightmare?
- Would businesses benefit from a single economic system?
- Would Canadians gain or lose financially?
- And would Canada suddenly be on the hook for U.S. national debt?

Let's follow the money and see if this deal makes financial sense—or if both countries would need an economic therapist.

1. U.S. Debt vs. Canadian Stability – Would Canada Inherit America's Trillions in Debt?

Let's start with the elephant in the room (or rather, the trillion-dollar debt crisis in the room).

The U.S. national debt is over $34 trillion and growing every day. (That's "trillion" with a "T"—as in, "Too Much Money to Ever Pay Off.")

Canada, on the other hand, has a much lower national debt—around $1.2 trillion USD.

So what happens if Canada joins the U.S.?

- Does Canada inherit part of the U.S. debt? (A very expensive "Welcome to America" gift.)
- Would Canada's economic stability help offset U.S. debt, or would it just get swallowed up?
- Would the U.S. be forced to address its debt crisis if Canada became a state? (Spoiler: Probably not.)

Would Canadians Accept U.S.-Style Deficit Spending?

Canada has a reputation for being fiscally responsible (well, more responsible than the U.S., anyway).

- The U.S. government spends more than it makes every year.
- Canada's government spends less aggressively and generally tries to balance its budgets over time.

Would Canadians be comfortable joining a system that runs on massive debt and deficit spending?

Or would Canada's more cautious approach to budgeting help stabilize the U.S. economy? (Ha, imagine a Canadian accountant lecturing Congress on responsible spending!)

2. Impact on Key Industries – Who Wins and Who Loses?

If Canada became part of the U.S., some industries would thrive, while others might struggle to adjust.

Oil & Gas – Would Alberta Love It or Hate It?

Alberta's economy is heavily dependent on oil & gas, making it Canada's version of Texas—but with more snow and fewer cowboy hats.

- In the U.S., energy policy changes dramatically depending on which party is in power.
- Alberta has clashed with Canada's federal government over environmental policies—would it prefer the U.S. approach to energy?
- Would the U.S. become even more energy independent with Alberta's oil reserves?

Biggest concern for Alberta: Could U.S. environmental regulations become more restrictive, making it harder to export oil?

(Expect Alberta to negotiate hard for its energy interests before signing any statehood deal!)

Banking & Financial Institutions – Can Canada's Stable Banks Survive the U.S. System?

Canada's banking system is one of the most stable in the world.

- The U.S. banking system is more free-market-driven, meaning banks can take bigger risks (and bigger losses).

- Canada's banks are highly regulated, meaning they avoid major crashes—like the 2008 financial crisis that hit the U.S. hard.

- If Canada joined the U.S., would Canadian banks be forced to deregulate?

Biggest Risk: Would Canada's banks lose their stability by being forced into America's high-risk, high-reward financial system?

Or would Canada's approach influence the U.S. to tighten its financial regulations? (Not likely, but fun to imagine!)

3. Trade & Business Integration – Does NAFTA/USMCA Even Matter Anymore?

The U.S. and Canada are already each other's largest trading partners.

Over $600 billion in goods and services flow between the two countries every year.

If Canada became a U.S. state:

- Would we even need NAFTA/USMCA anymore? (Why have a trade deal between two halves of the same country?)

- Would Canadian businesses gain better access to the U.S. market, or would they face more competition?

- Would cross-border supply chains become simpler, or would statehood create new regulations to deal with?

Biggest Business Question: Would U.S. companies flood into Canada's economy, buying up local businesses?

(Expect major debates over corporate takeovers, especially in industries like telecom, media, and natural resources!)

4. Would Canadians Lose or Gain Financially?

Let's get personal—how would individual Canadians be affected financially?

* Possible Financial Wins for Canadians:
- Lower income taxes (but at the cost of fewer social services).
- More access to U.S. investment markets and business opportunities.
- No more exchange rate issues when traveling to the U.S. (finally, everything costs what it actually says on the price tag!).

* Possible Financial Losses for Canadians:
- Higher healthcare costs (say goodbye to free doctor visits!).
- Higher education costs (university tuition could skyrocket).
- Fewer social benefits (like paid parental leave and stronger unemployment insurance).

Would the Average Canadian See a Pay Raise or Pay Cut?

- Some industries (tech, energy, and finance) could see wage increases due to U.S. labor demand.
- Other sectors (public services, education, and healthcare) could see pay cuts due to lower government spending.
- Would Canadian businesses move their headquarters to U.S. cities for tax reasons?

In short: Some people would benefit financially, while others would lose out.

Would the economic disruption be worth it? That's the trillion-dollar question.

Final Thoughts: Is This Merger Financially Feasible?

Biggest Economic Wins:
* Stronger North American trade integration.
* More economic opportunities for businesses.
* Easier cross-border transactions and labor mobility.

Biggest Economic Risks:
* Would Canada's stable economy be overwhelmed by U.S. debt?
* Would social benefits like healthcare and retirement funds survive?
* Would Canada's strong banking system weaken under U.S. financial regulations?

Would this be an economic superpower move, or would both countries struggle to adapt?

Would Canada gain economic freedom, or would it become just another U.S. state with no special financial advantages?

| 19 |

Immigration Policies

Canada's immigration system is vastly different from the U.S. model. Would this change cause border chaos, or could it create a smoother immigration process for both countries?

Main Points & Objectives:
- Canada's Immigration System: Points-Based vs. U.S. Lottery & Family-Based
    - Canada prioritizes skilled workers
    - The U.S. prioritizes family reunification and diversity visas
- Border Security Changes
    - Would the U.S.-Canada border even exist anymore?
    - Would Canada have to adopt stricter U.S. border policies?
- What Happens to Canadian Permanent Residents?
    - Would PRs automatically gain U.S. citizenship?
    - Could Canada's statehood affect global immigration trends?
- Impact on Refugee & Asylum Policies
    - Canada is much more open to refugees than the U.S.
    - Would new U.S. states follow federal policies or create their own?

Fun Fact: In 2018, more Americans immigrated to Canada than ever before due to political tensions in the U.S.—would this trend reverse if Canada became a state?

Would Statehood Open the Border... or Just Create a New Immigration Mess?

Would Canada Keep Its Immigration System or Be Forced Into the U.S. Model?

One of the biggest changes in a U.S.-Canada merger wouldn't just be about taxes, laws, or Tim Hortons becoming the official coffee of America (though let's be honest, it should be).

It would be immigration.

The U.S. and Canada have completely different immigration systems—and if Canada became a U.S. state, it would create massive policy questions, such as:
- Would Canada's points-based system be replaced by the U.S. lottery and family-based system?
- Would the U.S.-Canada border even exist anymore?
- Would Canadian permanent residents suddenly become U.S. citizens?
- How would this impact global migration patterns?

Basically, this wouldn't just change Canada and the U.S.—it could reshape immigration worldwide.

Let's break it down.

1. Canada's Immigration System vs. The U.S. Model – Two Very Different Approaches

If Canada became a U.S. state, would it have to adopt the American immigration system?

Canada's Immigration Model – The Points System

* Canada prioritizes skilled workers—if you have the right qualifications, you get in.

* Points are awarded based on education, language skills, and job experience.

* The system is designed to attract workers who will boost the economy.

* Canada also has more generous refugee policies compared to the U.S.

U.S. Immigration Model – Family-Based & Lottery System

* The U.S. focuses more on family reunification—immigrants can sponsor relatives.

* There's also a diversity visa lottery—basically a green card raffle.

* The system is harder to navigate, with long wait times and strict quotas.

* The U.S. has stricter refugee policies than Canada.

Biggest Policy Question: Would Canada Keep Its Immigration System?

- Would Canadian provinces be allowed to keep their points-based immigration system?

- Or would all immigration decisions be controlled by Washington, D.C.?

- Would America adopt some Canadian-style policies to attract skilled workers? (That would be an interesting plot twist!)

(If Canada's system stayed in place, expect U.S. tech companies to start demanding a "points-based" system for themselves!)

2. Border Security – Would the U.S.-Canada Border Even Exist Anymore?

Right now, the U.S.-Canada border is the longest undefended border in the world—over 5,500 miles of polite handshakes, duty-free shops, and the occasional moose wandering into traffic.

But if Canada became part of the U.S.:
- Would the border even exist anymore?
- Would Canadians and Americans have total free movement, like in the European Union?
- Would former border towns suddenly become like "Kansas and Missouri"—just another state-to-state crossing?

Potential Border Changes:
* No more border checkpoints? Canadians could freely move to any U.S. state.
* More integrated trade & business opportunities with no customs delays.
* Traveling between Toronto and New York would be as easy as driving from Boston to Philadelphia.

But There's a Catch...
* The U.S. has stricter border policies than Canada.
* Would Canada have to adopt U.S.-style immigration security? (More border walls? More ICE agents?)
* Would Canadians be okay inheriting American border policies—including stricter visa rules for travelers from certain countries?

Fun Fact: There are actually towns on the U.S.-Canada border where the border runs through houses and libraries. Would those borderlines just disappear overnight?

3. What Happens to Canadian Permanent Residents?

Would Canadian PRs (permanent residents) automatically become U.S. citizens?

Right now, Canada has millions of immigrants with PR status—people who:
* Have the right to live and work in Canada.
* Are on track for Canadian citizenship.
* Enjoy Canadian social benefits but aren't full citizens.

But if Canada became part of the U.S.:
- Would all PRs automatically get U.S. green cards?
- Would they be fast-tracked to U.S. citizenship?
- Or would they suddenly have to follow U.S. immigration rules—making it harder for them to stay?

(Expect massive protests if PRs suddenly had to "start over" in the U.S. system!)

4. Impact on Refugee & Asylum Policies – Would Canada's Open-Door Policy Survive?

Canada has a much more open refugee policy than the U.S.—it takes in more asylum seekers per capita and has faster processing times.

If Canada became a U.S. state:
- Would refugees trying to enter Canada now have to apply through the U.S. system?
- Would Canada's more welcoming policy disappear?
- Would Canadian states try to pass their own immigration laws, like California does?

Would Refugees Start Choosing a Different Country?

- Right now, many refugees and immigrants apply to Canada because it's easier than the U.S.

- If Canada's system disappeared, would they start choosing Europe or Australia instead?

- Could this shift global migration patterns in unpredictable ways?

(If Canada lost its reputation as an immigration-friendly country, it could change how people move around the world!)

5. Would Americans Start Moving to Canada... or Would Canadians Move South?

Fun Fact: In 2018, more Americans immigrated to Canada than ever before due to political tensions in the U.S.

But if Canada became a U.S. state:

- Would those Americans who moved north suddenly become U.S. citizens again?

- Would more Americans start moving to Canada's former provinces? (Imagine Americans "moving to Ontario for better healthcare"—what a twist!)

- Would Canadians start moving south to escape higher living costs?

Would this completely reshape North American migration patterns?

Final Thoughts: Would This Make Immigration Easier... or More Complicated?

Biggest Wins for Immigration:

* No more U.S.-Canada border—travel and trade would be easier than ever.

* Workers could move freely between Canadian and American cities.

* Businesses would benefit from a shared labor market.

Biggest Risks for Immigration:

* Canada's points-based system could disappear.

* U.S. border security policies could take over.

* Canadian provinces might lose control over their own immigration policies.

* Refugees and asylum seekers could face more obstacles.

Would Canada's immigration model survive?

Would Americans start moving to Canada's new U.S. states for better jobs and healthcare?

Or would Canada be forced into the U.S. system, making immigration more complicated than ever?

One thing's for sure: This wouldn't just be a policy change—it would be a total migration shake-up.

| 20 |

Currency and Banking

Canada has the Canadian dollar (CAD), while the U.S. uses the American dollar (USD). Would Canada have to switch currencies, and what economic impact would this have?

Main Points & Objectives:
- The U.S. Dollar vs. Canadian Dollar
- CAD fluctuates based on oil prices, while USD is a global reserve currency
- Would Canadian businesses benefit from a stronger currency?
- Would Canadians Have to Exchange Their Money?
- Could they transition seamlessly, or would it create inflation concerns?
- How Would This Impact Trade & Investment?
- U.S. investors would no longer have to worry about exchange rates
- Canadian pension funds would have to adjust investments
- Would Banks Merge?
- Canada has a more regulated banking system than the U.S.
- Could major Canadian banks (RBC, TD, Scotiabank) merge with U.S. institutions?

Fun Fact: The U.S. once printed two-dollar bills—Canada still does, but they're called "Toonies" (a $2 coin). Would Canada's iconic currency disappear?

Would Canada's Beloved Loonie Be Sent Into Retirement?

Would Canada Keep Its Currency, or Would It Be All About the Benjamins?

If Canada became a U.S. state, one of the first practical economic questions would be:

Would Canada keep the Canadian dollar (CAD), or would it switch to the U.S. dollar (USD)?

While this might seem like a technical issue, it would actually have massive economic consequences for businesses, consumers, and even Canada's cultural identity.

Would Canadians gain from a stronger currency—or would they feel like they were losing a part of their heritage?

Let's dive into the financial, economic, and cultural impacts of saying goodbye to the Loonie.

1. The U.S. Dollar vs. The Canadian Dollar – What's the Difference?

The U.S. dollar (USD) and Canadian dollar (CAD) might look similar (except for the fact that Canadian money is way more colorful and waterproof!), but they function very differently in global markets.

The U.S. Dollar (USD):

* The world's dominant reserve currency—used in international trade and finance.

* Backed by the world's largest economy and strongest financial institutions.

* More stable—even in economic downturns, it remains strong.

* Used in dozens of countries as an unofficial second currency.

The Canadian Dollar (CAD):

* More tied to oil prices—when oil is strong, CAD rises; when oil drops, CAD weakens.

* Used only in Canada—not a global reserve currency.

* More regulated banking system, leading to greater financial stability.

* Has a cool nickname ("the Loonie") and fun, colorful banknotes.

Biggest Issue: Would Canada's Economy Benefit or Struggle If It Adopted the U.S. Dollar?

- Would Canadian businesses benefit from a stronger currency?
- Would exports suffer if the Canadian dollar disappeared?
- Would Canadians lose their ability to control their own financial policies?

(And, most importantly—would the "Loonie" and "Toonie" disappear?)

2. Would Canadians Have to Exchange Their Money?

Scenario A: A Seamless Transition (Best-Case Scenario)
If Canada smoothly adopted the U.S. dollar:

* Banks would automatically convert all Canadian accounts into U.S. dollars.

* Canadians wouldn't need to exchange money manually—it would happen electronically.

* Businesses would gradually price everything in U.S. dollars instead of CAD.

This would be like when European countries switched to the Euro—a temporary hassle, but manageable.

Scenario B: Financial Chaos (Worst-Case Scenario)
If the transition was poorly managed:
* Prices could fluctuate wildly as businesses adjust.
* Inflation could spike if the transition caused economic instability.
* Consumers and businesses might lose money during currency exchanges.

(And let's be real—Canadians would definitely be mad if they lost money in the switch!)

3. How Would This Impact Trade & Investment?

Canada and the U.S. already trade over $600 billion per year.

- Right now, businesses have to deal with exchange rate fluctuations—sometimes the CAD is worth more, sometimes less.
- If Canada switched to the U.S. dollar:
* No more exchange rate worries—trade becomes simpler.
* Investment from the U.S. could increase since businesses wouldn't need to convert money.
* Tourists wouldn't have to do mental math when visiting Niagara Falls.

But There's a Catch...
- Canadian businesses would lose the ability to devalue their currency to stay competitive in global markets.

- Export-heavy industries (like oil & lumber) could suffer if the stronger U.S. dollar makes their products more expensive.

Would Canada gain economic stability from switching currencies—or would it lose financial flexibility?

(Economists would have a field day debating this!)

4. Would Banks Merge?

Canada's banking system is very different from the U.S.

- Canada has fewer, but more regulated, banks (RBC, TD, Scotiabank, etc.).
- The U.S. has more banks, but with looser regulations and a history of financial crashes.

What Would Happen If the Two Systems Merged?

- Would Canada's strict banking regulations weaken under U.S. policies?
- Would big American banks buy out Canadian institutions?
- Or would Canada's banking system actually influence the U.S. to be more stable?

Fun Fact: Canada's banking system avoided the 2008 financial crisis better than the U.S.—could Canada's influence help prevent future economic meltdowns?

(If Canada's banking regulations survived, expect Wall Street to throw a fit!)

5. Would Canadians Lose or Gain Financially?

Possible Financial Wins for Canadians:

* Easier trade & travel with the U.S.

* More investment opportunities as Canada becomes part of a bigger economy.

* Stronger currency means more purchasing power abroad.

Possible Financial Losses for Canadians:

* Loss of economic sovereignty—Canadians wouldn't control their own currency.

* Higher prices for exports, hurting industries like oil and agriculture.

* Banking deregulation could make financial crises more likely.

Would Canada's economic security improve under the U.S. dollar, or would it be a risky move?

6. Would Canada Keep Any Unique Coins or Bills?

Cultural Impact of Losing the Loonie & Toonie

- Canadians love their unique money—it's colorful, fun, and has national identity.

- If Canada adopted U.S. money:

* No more Loonie or Toonie.

* No more hockey players or polar bears on banknotes.

* No more Queen Elizabeth or King Charles on Canadian bills.

Would Canadians Fight to Keep Their Coins?

What if Canadian provinces kept their coins as a regional tradition? (Imagine a "Loonie token" you could use at Tim Hortons but nowhere else!)

Or would Canada become just another state with plain, green U.S. bills?

(If this happens, expect an emotional outcry from Canadians!).

Final Thoughts: Would Canada's Currency Survive?

Biggest Wins for Canada:
* Simpler trade & investment with the U.S.
* No more exchange rate worries for businesses.
* Stronger, more stable currency.

Biggest Risks for Canada:
* Loss of economic independence.
* Risk of banking deregulation and financial instability.
* Cultural loss—no more Loonie or Toonie!

Biggest Wins for the U.S.:
* Stronger North American economic integration.
* Fewer exchange rate issues.
* Increased investment from Canadian businesses.

Biggest Risks for the U.S.:
* Would Canada's more regulated banking system interfere with Wall Street?
* Would the transition create short-term economic instability?

Would Canadians be willing to give up their currency for the economic benefits?

Or would they fight to keep the Loonie alive—even if it meant a separate banking system?

One thing's for sure: This wouldn't just be an economic change—it would be a cultural one, too.

| 21 |

How Could Canada Actually Become a U.S. State?

I f Canada wanted to do this, how would it actually happen?
      - Key Topics:
    - Step 1: National referendum in Canada
    - Step 2: U.S. Congress approval
    - Step 3: Constitutional amendments
    - Step 4: Transition phase (new laws, currency, military integration, etc.)
    - Fun Fact: Hawaii took 60 years from becoming a U.S. territory to achieving full statehood. Would Canada take longer or shorter?

Here's the fully developed outline for Chapters 22-24, expanding on Part V: Real-World Feasibility and Implementation.

Would This Be a Smooth Process… or Take Longer Than a Canadian Winter?

If Canada Wanted to Join the U.S., What Would It Take?

So, after all the political debates, economic discussions, and endless poutine-fueled arguments, let's assume Canada decides to go for it.

The big question now is:

How do you actually turn a sovereign nation into a U.S. state (or multiple states)?

Spoiler alert: It's not as simple as swearing an oath, changing road signs to miles, and replacing the Queen with George Washington.

This process would involve legal battles, political negotiations, and enough paperwork to make even the most seasoned bureaucrat cry.

But, in theory, it could be done. Here's how it might play out—step by step.

Step 1: National Referendum in Canada – Do Canadians Even Want This?

Before anything happens, Canada has to decide if it actually wants to join the U.S. (Because forcing Canada in would be, well... let's just say history hasn't been kind to forced annexations.)

How It Would Work:
- Parliament would call for a national vote (similar to Brexit).
- A simple majority (50%+1) would be needed for approval.
- Every province would vote separately—but would it be an "all or nothing" deal, or could some provinces join while others stay in Canada?

Potential Challenges:
- Quebec would almost certainly vote no.
- Alberta might push hard for statehood.
- Would provinces negotiate their own deals with the U.S.?

(If this referendum was anything like Brexit, expect years of political chaos and family dinner arguments.)

Step 2: U.S. Congress Approval – Does America Want This?

Let's say Canadians vote YES (or at least enough provinces do). Now, the U.S. has to decide:

Would Congress even approve Canada's statehood bid?

Legal Requirement:
According to Article IV, Section 3 of the U.S. Constitution, new states can be admitted...
* If Congress approves.
* If existing states agree.

Challenges in Congress:
- Would Republicans worry that Canada's liberal-leaning provinces would tilt the Senate?
- Would Democrats worry about adding conservative regions like Alberta?
- Would some states fear losing influence if Canada became a political powerhouse?

(Expect heated Senate debates, partisan gridlock, and plenty of grandstanding on cable news.)

Fun Fact: Hawaii had to wait 60 years after becoming a U.S. territory before achieving statehood. Would Canada take longer—or would Congress fast-track it?

Step 3: Constitutional Amendments – Changing the Rules of the Game

This is where things get legally messy.

Would adding Canada require a constitutional amendment?

Possible Issues:
- Would Canada join as one giant state... or multiple new states?
- Would this shift the balance of power in the U.S. Senate?
- Would Canada need special protections for things like bilingual laws (English/French)?

Scenario A: No Constitutional Amendment Needed
- If Congress simply votes to admit Canada, the process is straight-forward.
- Canada would be subject to existing U.S. laws and constitutional rules.

Scenario B: Constitutional Amendments Required
- If Canada wanted exceptions (e.g., keeping universal healthcare, different gun laws, stronger Indigenous rights protections), the U.S. Constitution might need changes.
- Constitutional amendments require approval from two-thirds of Congress and three-fourths of U.S. states—which is extremely diffi-cult to achieve.

(Would Americans really agree to change their Constitution just for Canada?)

Step 4: Transition Phase – Adapting to U.S. Laws, Currency, and Military

Even after the legal process is settled, the actual transition would take years—if not decades.

Legal & Political Adjustments

- Canadian laws would have to align with U.S. federal law.
- Courts would transition to the American legal system (goodbye, Queen's Bench, hello, Supreme Court!).
- Gun laws, tax laws, and healthcare policies would need serious negotiations.

Currency & Economy Adjustments
- Would Canada keep the Loonie or adopt the U.S. dollar?
- Would Canadian banks merge with U.S. financial institutions?
- Would the cost of living rise or fall for Canadians?

Military & Defense
- Would Canada's military merge with the U.S. Armed Forces?
- Would Canadian bases become U.S. military outposts?
- Would Canada be required to increase military spending?

(Imagine Canada suddenly having U.S. nuclear weapons on its soil—would Canadians be okay with that?)

How Long Would This Process Take?

Historical Reference:
- Hawaii took 60 years from becoming a U.S. territory to achieving full statehood.
- Texas was an independent country for 9 years before joining the U.S.
- Puerto Rico has been waiting for statehood for decades.

Best-Case Scenario: 10-20 Years
- If everything went smoothly, Canada could fully integrate within a decade or two.

Worst-Case Scenario: 50+ Years

- If statehood triggered major legal battles, political fights, and economic adjustments, the process could take half a century—or never happen at all.

(In other words, if this were a Netflix show, we'd be on Season 30 before Canada officially became a state.)

Final Thoughts: Could This Actually Happen?

Biggest Obstacles:
* Would Canadians actually vote for this?
* Would the U.S. Congress approve it?
* Would the process take so long that the idea dies before completion?

Biggest Opportunities:
* Canada and the U.S. could form a stronger economic powerhouse.
* Trade and travel between both countries would be easier than ever.
* A unified North America could have more global influence.

Most Likely Outcome?
It's possible—but extremely unlikely. The legal and political hurdles would be monumental.

But hey—if history has taught us anything, it's that stranger things have happened.

Would Canadians be willing to go through this long, complex process for statehood?

Or would they just say "Nah, we're good, eh."

| 22 |

International Reactions

The U.S. and Canada have long been seen as two distinct nations with strong alliances, but how would the rest of the world react if Canada became a U.S. state? Would global superpowers approve, or would they see it as an expansionist move by the U.S.?

Main Points & Objectives:
- How Would the United Nations (UN) Respond?
- Canada is a respected independent voice in international diplomacy.
- Would the UN approve of a peaceful merger, or would it see it as U.S. expansionism?
- Could Canada's existing treaties and diplomatic agreements still apply?
- How Would NATO and Other Allies React?
- Both countries are NATO members—would it make NATO stronger?
- Would Canada lose its separate voice in military diplomacy?
- Could other NATO members see this as the U.S. gaining too much power?
- Would Other Countries Oppose It?
- China & Russia might oppose, seeing it as an expansion of U.S. influence.
- European Union (EU)—would they lose a key trade partner?

- Mexico—could this disrupt the balance of North American relations?

- What Happens to Canada's Role in the Commonwealth?

- Canada is a Commonwealth nation under the British monarchy—what happens to its relationship with the UK?

- Would Queen Elizabeth II (or now King Charles III) be okay with losing one of her realms?

Fun Fact: Canada and the U.S. are so closely aligned that in 2019, a global survey found that many people in Europe thought Canada was already a U.S. state!

Would the World See This as a Friendly Merger... or a U.S. Power Grab?

How Would the World React to Canada Becoming a U.S. State?

If Canada officially became part of the U.S., it wouldn't just be a North American issue—it would be a global shockwave.

- Would world leaders support it, or see it as American expansionism?

- Would Canada lose its independent voice on the world stage?

- Would allies like NATO and the UK approve, or would they be furious?

- And what would countries like China and Russia have to say about it?

Let's take a deep dive into the world's response—because, trust me, the global reaction would be bigger than when Canadians found out Tim Hortons changed their coffee recipe. (A true national crisis!).

1. How Would the United Nations (UN) Respond?

Right now, Canada is an independent country with a respected voice in the UN.

It's known for being:
* A neutral peacekeeping nation that isn't seen as overly aggressive.
* A major player in climate policy, human rights, and international trade.
* A country with independent relationships with global powers like China, India, and the EU.

If Canada became a U.S. state, the UN might have some concerns:
- Would Canada lose its separate vote at the UN? (Right now, it has an equal say—would that disappear?)
- Would Canada's independent foreign policy vanish, making it just an extension of U.S. interests?
- Would the UN see this as a peaceful democratic process, or as a U.S. territorial expansion?

Historical Comparison: When East and West Germany reunited in 1990, East Germany lost its UN seat and diplomatic independence—would the same thing happen to Canada?

(Let's just say that UN diplomats would have A LOT to talk about over coffee.)

2. How Would NATO and Other Military Allies React?

Canada and the U.S. are both founding members of NATO—so they already work closely together militarily.

If Canada became a U.S. state, would it strengthen NATO or disrupt it?

* Potential Benefits for NATO:

- Canada's military would fully integrate into the U.S. Armed Forces.

- Joint military operations would be simpler—no more cross-border logistics.

- Canada's Arctic defenses would merge with U.S. security strategy.

* Potential Problems for NATO:

- Would Canada lose its independent voice in military diplomacy?

- Would European NATO members worry that the U.S. is becoming too dominant?

- Would other NATO countries (like France or Germany) feel uneasy about the U.S. growing even larger?

Worst-Case Scenario: Could this actually cause tension in NATO? Some countries already worry that the U.S. has too much control—would Canada's statehood tip the balance even more?

(If there's one thing European leaders hate, it's feeling like the U.S. is making all the decisions.)

3. Would Other Countries Oppose It?

Not every country would be happy about this.

China & Russia – The Biggest Opponents?

- Both China and Russia already worry about U.S. influence expanding.

- If Canada joined the U.S., it would dramatically increase America's size, resources, and strategic Arctic presence.

- Russia, in particular, might see this as a direct geopolitical threat (especially with Arctic competition heating up).

Fun Fact: The U.S. and Canada already share NORAD (North American Aerospace Defense Command), but if Canada became a U.S. state, the Arctic would become fully American-controlled. (Something Russia would NOT be thrilled about!).

The European Union (EU) – Would They Lose a Key Trade Partner?
- Canada has a strong trade relationship with the EU under agreements like CETA (Comprehensive Economic and Trade Agreement).
- Would those agreements survive if Canada became part of the U.S.?
- Would the EU feel like it lost a neutral diplomatic ally and gained another American-controlled economy?

(The EU already struggles with U.S. economic dominance—losing Canada might make them even grumpier!)

Mexico – Would This Disrupt North American Relations?
- Right now, Canada and Mexico have a strong bilateral relationship—but would Mexico feel uneasy about being left alone as the only non-U.S. country in North America?
- Would the U.S. shift its trade focus to Canada, leaving Mexico behind?
- Would this change affect NAFTA/USMCA agreements?

(Would Mexico suddenly feel like a third wheel at the North American dinner table?)

4. What Happens to Canada's Role in the Commonwealth?

Canada is a Commonwealth nation, meaning it recognizes the British monarchy.

But if Canada became a U.S. state... what happens to King Charles III's influence?

Three Possible Outcomes:

1. Canada Completely Leaves the Commonwealth – Would King Charles lose Canada as one of his realms? (That would definitely annoy the Royal Family.)

2. Canada Stays in the Commonwealth as a U.S. State – Could Canada still have a symbolic relationship with the UK? (Unlikely—no U.S. state has ever been part of the Commonwealth.)

3. The UK Tries to Stop the Transition – Would the British government oppose Canada leaving the monarchy? (Would they have a legal argument, or just be salty about it?)

Historical Example: When India and South Africa left the British Empire, it changed the entire dynamic of the Commonwealth—would Canada's departure have a similar impact?

(Let's just say Buckingham Palace wouldn't be throwing a party over this news.)

Final Thoughts: Would the World Approve or Protest?

Biggest Supporters:
* The U.S. itself (if Congress approved it).
* Some NATO members who want stronger North American military cooperation.
* U.S. businesses eager for an even larger economic empire.

Biggest Opponents:
* China and Russia, seeing this as a U.S. expansionist move.
* The EU, worried about losing an independent trade partner.
* The UK, frustrated that Canada might leave the Commonwealth.

The Biggest Question: Would This Change the Balance of Global Power?

- Would this make the U.S. an unstoppable global force?
- Would it create diplomatic rifts with allies who prefer an independent Canada?
- Would the world react with applause... or sanctions?

One thing's for sure—this would be one of the biggest geopolitical shifts of the 21st century.

Would Canada becoming a U.S. state be seen as a peaceful, voluntary move?

Or would the world freak out and start sounding the alarm on American expansionism?

| 23 |

Could Canada be Multiple U.S. States?

With ten provinces and three territories, could Canada become multiple U.S. states instead of just one? This chapter explores whether provinces would join separately or as a single entity.

Main Points & Objectives:
- Could Canada Join as One State or Multiple?
- If Canada joined as one state, it would have more people than Texas, Florida, and New York combined!
- If each province became its own state, Canada could add 10+ new states to the U.S.!
- Province-by-Province Breakdown:
- British Columbia (BC): Strong economy, would fit well with U.S. Pacific states like Washington and Oregon.
- Alberta & Saskatchewan: Conservative, resource-heavy economies—likely to lean Republican.
- Manitoba & Ontario: Economic hubs, politically moderate—would be swing states.
- Quebec: Major cultural & language differences—would it demand special autonomy or independence instead?
- Atlantic Provinces (Nova Scotia, New Brunswick, Newfoundland, PEI): Small populations, but strong maritime economy.

- Northern Territories (Yukon, Northwest Territories, Nunavut): Would they remain federally managed like U.S. territories (Guam, Puerto Rico)?
  - Would This Shift the U.S. Political Balance?
  - More states = More Senators & House Representatives.
  - Could Canada change the outcome of future U.S. elections?

Fun Fact: If Canada were split into separate states, it would instantly create the largest number of new U.S. states since the 19th century!

Would Canada Join as One Super-State... or Become America's Newest Statehood Bonanza?

Would Canada Join as One State or Be Divided into Many?

If Canada became part of the U.S., one of the biggest questions would be:

- Would it join as a single state (making it the second-most populous in America)?
- Would each province become its own state (potentially creating 10+ new states)?
- What happens to the three northern territories—would they become states or U.S. territories like Puerto Rico?

This isn't just a bureaucratic issue—it's a political and economic game-changer that could shift the balance of power in the U.S. Senate and House of Representatives.

Let's break it down province by province and see which ones would be swing states, conservative strongholds, or liberal bastions.

1. British Columbia (BC) – The California of the North?

Nickname: The West Coast Wild Card
Economy: Tech, film, tourism, forestry
Likely Political Leaning: Democratic (Liberal)

Would BC Fit in as a U.S. State?
* Culturally and economically aligned with Washington, Oregon, and California—West Coast states with strong tech, environmental policies, and progressive politics.
* Massive trade hub with Asia—Vancouver is a key port city.
* Thriving film industry (Hollywood North)—would the U.S. finally give Canada credit for making half its movies?

Biggest Issue: BC has a strong environmental movement—would it clash with U.S. federal energy policies?

2. Alberta – The Texas of the North?

Nickname: Little Texas
Economy: Oil & gas, agriculture, tech
Likely Political Leaning: Republican (Conservative)

Would Alberta Fit in as a U.S. State?
* Culturally similar to Texas and Oklahoma—big on oil, lower taxes, and strong conservative values.
* Already has secessionist movements—some Albertans have joked about joining the U.S. anyway!
* Would strengthen America's energy industry—Texas would finally have a northern oil buddy.

Biggest Issue: Would Alberta demand special autonomy for its energy policies (imagine the debates over U.S. environmental regulations!).

3. Saskatchewan – The Underrated Powerhouse

Nickname: America's Future Breadbasket
Economy: Agriculture, mining, energy
Likely Political Leaning: Republican (Conservative)

Would Saskatchewan Fit in as a U.S. State?
* Strong rural economy—a perfect match for Midwestern states like Nebraska or Kansas.
* Massive natural resources—would strengthen U.S. food and energy security.
* Low population, big landmass—perfect for anyone looking for wide-open spaces (Wyoming, meet your new best friend!).

Biggest Issue: Would Saskatchewan's farmers adapt to U.S. agricultural subsidies and trade policies?

4. Manitoba – The Swing State in the Making

Nickname: The Middle Ground
Economy: Agriculture, manufacturing, finance
Likely Political Leaning: Swing State

Would Manitoba Fit in as a U.S. State?
* Moderate, balanced politics—could be a swing state like Wisconsin or Pennsylvania.
* Key trade and transportation hub—Winnipeg is a major shipping center.
* Blends urban and rural interests, making it a bellwether state in U.S. elections.

Biggest Issue: Would Manitoba's strong Indigenous communities lose legal protections under U.S. law?

5. Ontario – The New York of the North?

Nickname: The Economic Powerhouse
Economy: Finance, tech, auto industry
Likely Political Leaning: Democratic (Liberal)

Would Ontario Fit in as a U.S. State?
* Massive economic center—would be the second-largest economy of any U.S. state (after California).
* Politically similar to states like New York and Illinois—leaning center-left.
* Toronto would be America's fourth-largest city, adding major influence in elections.

Biggest Issue: Would Ontario lose its financial independence under U.S. regulations?

6. Quebec – The Wild Card (Would It Even Join?)

Nickname: The Lone Wolf
Economy: Aerospace, energy, culture
Likely Political Leaning: Unknown – Might Not Even Join!

Would Quebec Fit in as a U.S. State?
- Highly unlikely. Quebec has a strong separatist movement and would likely demand special autonomy—or outright refuse to join the U.S. at all.

Biggest Issues:
- Language barrier—would Quebec demand French as an official U.S. language?
- Cultural independence—would it negotiate for its own legal system?
- Could it stay independent instead?

(If Quebec did join, expect a LOT of French lessons in American schools!).

7. Atlantic Canada – Would They Join Together or Separately?

Nicknames: The Maritimes & Newfoundland
Economy: Fishing, energy, tourism
Likely Political Leaning: Swing Region

Would Atlantic Canada Fit in as U.S. States?
* Close economic ties to the U.S. already.
* Would benefit from easier trade and tourism.
* Might form a single state for efficiency.

Biggest Issue: Would they lose control over their fisheries and energy policies under U.S. regulations?

8. The Northern Territories – Would They Become U.S. States or Territories?

Nicknames: The Arctic Trio (Yukon, Northwest Territories, Nunavut)
Economy: Mining, Indigenous governance, Arctic security
Likely Political Leaning: Undetermined – Special Status?

Would the Territories Become States or Stay as U.S. Territories?
- The U.S. has territories like Puerto Rico and Guam—would the northern territories have a similar status?
- Would Nunavut keep Indigenous self-governance?
- Would the U.S. take a stronger role in Arctic affairs?

(Fun fact: Nunavut is larger than Texas, California, and Montana combined!).

Final Thoughts: Would Canada Be One State or Many?

Scenario 1: Canada Becomes One Giant State
* Simple transition process.
* Easier for governance.
* Would have too much power in Congress—likely unrealistic.

Scenario 2: Each Province Becomes Its Own State
* More Senate and House representation.
* Gives provinces more autonomy.
* Would dramatically shift U.S. political power.

Scenario 3: A Mix – Some States, Some Territories
* Quebec could remain independent or semi-autonomous.
* The Northern Territories might stay as U.S. territories.
* Provinces could choose their fate.

Would this be the biggest expansion of U.S. states in history?

Or would the complexity of dividing Canada kill the idea altogether?

| 24 |

Potential Timeline: How Long Would This Take?

Even if Canada wanted to become a U.S. state, it wouldn't happen overnight. This chapter outlines a realistic timeline of events and the legal, political, and economic steps that would need to take place.

Main Points & Objectives:
- Phase 1: Public Discourse & National Referendum (Years 1-3)
- Would require nationwide debates, political campaigns, and voting.
- Canadian citizens would have to approve statehood via referendum.
- Would there be resistance from political leaders or provinces like Quebec?
- Phase 2: U.S. Congressional Approval (Years 3-5)
- Congress must vote to accept new states.
- The U.S. could demand constitutional changes before admitting Canada.
- Would it require a two-thirds majority in both houses?
- Phase 3: Legal & Economic Integration (Years 5-10)
- Currency change (shifting from the Canadian dollar to the U.S. dollar).

- New state constitutions must be written (if provinces become states).
- Adjustment of military alliances, law enforcement, healthcare, and infrastructure.
- Phase 4: Full Integration & Political Representation (Years 10-15)
- First Canadian Senators & Representatives elected to U.S. Congress.
- Major laws adjusted to align with U.S. regulations.
- Final cultural and economic transitions completed.

Fun Fact: It took Hawaii over 60 years to transition from a U.S. territory to full statehood. Would Canada take longer or move faster?

Would Canada's Statehood Be a Fast Process... or Take Longer Than a Canadian Winter?

How Long Would It Take for Canada to Officially Join the U.S.?

Even if every Canadian woke up tomorrow and said, "Sure, let's become Americans," it wouldn't be instant.

This wouldn't be like downloading a new software update—it would be like upgrading an entire government, economy, and national identity.

Realistically, we're talking about a multi-decade process involving:
- Legal hurdles (lots of paperwork—lawyers would have a field day).
- Political negotiations (hello, Congress!).
- Economic shifts (goodbye, Canadian dollar?).
- Massive cultural and constitutional adjustments (would Canadians finally have to embrace the imperial system?).

So, let's break down the timeline phase by phase—because this process would take years, if not decades.

Phase 1: Public Discourse & National Referendum (Years 1-3)
Canadians Would Have to Vote First!

The first step in Canada's potential statehood journey wouldn't involve Washington, D.C.—it would start in Ottawa (and maybe in the nearest Tim Hortons).

Key Steps in Phase 1:
* National debate kicks off—politicians, economists, and citizens would all weigh in.
* Major political campaigns form—statehood advocates vs. sovereignty defenders.
* Provincial governments react—would some provinces push for their own deals?
* A national referendum is held—Canada would need 50%+1 of voters to say "yes."

Biggest Obstacles in Phase 1:
- Would Quebec even participate in the vote?
- Would certain provinces push for independence instead (looking at you, Alberta and Quebec)?
- Would Canada require a supermajority (more than 50%) to approve such a drastic change?

Fun Fact: The 1995 Quebec independence referendum failed by just 0.6%—meaning even tiny margins could make or break this decision.

Phase 2: U.S. Congressional Approval (Years 3-5)
Would the U.S. Even Say Yes?

Even if Canadians vote for statehood, it's not their decision alone. The U.S. Congress has the final say on admitting new states.

Key Steps in Phase 2:
* Congress debates the request—would it be one state or multiple?
* The Senate and House of Representatives vote—a simple majority in both is required.
* Possible constitutional changes—would amendments be needed to accommodate Canada's unique laws?
* Negotiations on political representation—how many Senators and Representatives would Canada get?

Biggest Obstacles in Phase 2:
- Would the U.S. see this as too risky politically?
- Would Republicans and Democrats fight over how this affects elections?
- Would existing states push back against adding such a massive new state(s)?

Fun Fact: Texas joined the U.S. as an independent republic, but it took nine years of negotiations! Would Canada's process be even longer?

Phase 3: Legal & Economic Integration (Years 5-10)
Changing Everything from Money to Military

Assuming Canada clears the U.S. political hurdles, the next challenge would be aligning laws, economics, and governance.

Economic Adjustments:
* The Canadian dollar would be phased out—a timeline for switching to USD would be set.
* Trade agreements like USMCA (formerly NAFTA) would become obsolete—trade barriers fully lifted.

* U.S. businesses would expand into Canada without needing international policies.

Legal Adjustments:
* Provinces would need state constitutions—similar to how Texas wrote one when it joined.
* Federal vs. state rights would be negotiated—would provinces keep unique laws (like stricter gun control)?
* Canadian courts would merge into the U.S. judicial system—goodbye, Supreme Court of Canada!

Military Adjustments:
* Canadian Armed Forces would integrate into the U.S. military.
* U.S. bases would expand northward—Alaska wouldn't feel so lonely anymore!
* NORAD (North American Aerospace Defense Command) operations would remain but under full U.S. control.

Biggest Obstacles in Phase 3:
- Would Canadians be okay with losing their unique banking and financial system?
- Would Quebec demand legal exceptions? (They probably would!).
- Would businesses struggle to adapt to new tax laws and federal oversight?

Fun Fact: When the Euro replaced national currencies in Europe, it took nearly 20 years of preparation—would Canada need a similar transition period for the U.S. dollar?

Phase 4: Full Integration & Political Representation (Years 10-15)
The First Canadian-American Elections!

The final stage of Canada's transition into the U.S. would be political integration.

Key Steps in Phase 4:
* The first U.S. elections featuring Canadian states would take place.
* Canada's Senators and Representatives take office in Washington, D.C.
* Final laws and regulations align with U.S. federal policies.
* State-level governance is fully operational.

Biggest Obstacles in Phase 4:
- Would Canadians adjust to the two-party U.S. political system?
- Would new Canadian states shift the balance of power in Congress?
- Would provinces that resisted the transition continue pushing for independence?

Fun Fact: When Alaska and Hawaii became states in 1959, their first U.S. Representatives had to quickly learn American political customs. Would Canadian politicians adapt smoothly—or would they struggle in Washington, D.C.?

Total Estimated Timeline: 10-20 Years (Or More!)

Best-Case Scenario: 10-15 Years
- If everything goes smoothly (which is highly unlikely), Canada could fully transition into the U.S. within a decade.

Realistic Scenario: 20+ Years
- Political battles, legal hurdles, and economic shifts could drag this process out for decades.
- Some provinces might resist, slowing down the transition even further.

- Cultural and financial debates could lead to delays or even reversals.

Historical Comparison:
- Hawaii took 60 years to transition from a U.S. territory to statehood.
- Puerto Rico has been debating statehood for decades, and it still hasn't happened.
- Texas took nine years of negotiations before joining in 1845.

(Translation: If Canada ever became part of the U.S., it would take a VERY long time!).

Final Thoughts: Is This Feasible or Just a Thought Experiment?

Biggest Reasons This Would Take Forever:
* Too many legal and political hurdles.
* Massive economic adjustments needed.
* Cultural and linguistic differences (hello, Quebec!).

Biggest Reasons It Could Happen Faster:
* If both governments aggressively pursued it, the process could be streamlined.
* If all provinces agreed on a uniform process.
* If global events pushed Canada toward U.S. alignment.

Would Canada becoming part of the U.S. be the biggest bureaucratic nightmare in history?

Or could it actually happen faster than expected—if the political will existed?

One thing's for sure: Even if Canadians and Americans agreed on this tomorrow, it wouldn't be official until AT LEAST 2040!

| 25 |

Case Studies: Lessons from Hawaii and Alaska

O ther places have gone through this before—what can we learn?

Key Topics:
  - Texas: How an independent country became a U.S. state
  - Hawaii: A sovereign kingdom turned into a state
  - Puerto Rico: Why it's still debating statehood today

Fun Fact: The Republic of Texas was once its own independent country before joining the U.S. in 1845—maybe Canada could follow a similar path?

What Can History Teach Us About Canada Joining the U.S.?

Could Canada Look to the Past for Guidance?

If Canada were to seriously consider joining the United States, it wouldn't be the first place in history to go through such a massive political transformation.

Throughout history, other territories, independent nations, and regions have gone through annexation, voluntary statehood, or extended political limbo.

So, what can Canada learn from these cases?
- Texas: An independent republic that voluntarily joined the U.S.
- Hawaii: A sovereign kingdom that was absorbed into America.
- Puerto Rico: A U.S. territory that still hasn't achieved statehood after more than 125 years.

Would Canada's journey mirror one of these cases, or be something completely new?

(Spoiler alert: It would probably be more complicated than all of them!).

1. Texas: The Lone Star Republic That Became a U.S. State

Nickname: The Original "Eh, Let's Join the U.S." Story
Status Before Statehood: Independent Republic (1836-1845)
How It Happened: Texas won independence from Mexico, ran itself for nearly a decade, and then asked to join the U.S.

Key Lessons from Texas:
* Independent nations can voluntarily join the U.S.—Texas set a precedent for peaceful annexation.
* The process took nearly a decade, showing that political and legal negotiations take time.
* It required balancing political power—Texas was a slave state, so its admission sparked controversy in Congress.

Biggest Differences from Canada:
- Texas was a small independent republic, not a major global player like Canada.

- Texas had fewer bureaucratic hurdles than a developed nation like Canada.

- Texas wanted to join the U.S. to gain military protection from Mexico—Canada doesn't have a similar security concern.

Would Canada follow Texas's path?

Maybe, but Texas was a tiny country compared to Canada. This approach would likely work only if Canada somehow became independent first. (And let's be honest—Quebec would love that part.).

2. Hawaii: From Sovereign Kingdom to U.S. State

Nickname: The Aloha (and Takeover) State

Status Before Statehood: Independent Kingdom (1795-1893), U.S. Territory (1898-1959)

How It Happened: American business interests overthrew the Hawaiian monarchy, and the U.S. annexed it despite local resistance.

Key Lessons from Hawaii:

* It shows that even sovereign nations can be absorbed into the U.S.

* It took decades to transition from a U.S. territory to full statehood (1898-1959).

* Cultural and political resistance can delay statehood—Hawaii had deep concerns over losing its native identity.

Biggest Differences from Canada:

- Hawaii's annexation was not fully voluntary—it involved a U.S.-backed coup against the Hawaiian monarchy.

- Hawaii had a much smaller population and was strategically valuable for the U.S. Navy.

- Canada has a strong democracy and would never allow a foreign-backed takeover. (Unless it was a hockey team trade gone horribly wrong).

Would Canada follow Hawaii's path?

Highly unlikely. Canada is too big, too independent, and too globally integrated to be annexed in such a way. However, Quebec might argue that statehood would destroy Canadian cultural identity—just as many Hawaiians argued in the 20th century.

(Translation: Expect some major protests from French-speaking Canadians!).

3. Puerto Rico: The Forever U.S. Territory That Can't Decide

Nickname: The Case of Perpetual Limbo
Status Before Statehood Debate: U.S. Territory since 1898
How It Happened: The U.S. took Puerto Rico from Spain in 1898, but it never became a state. Instead, it remains a territory with ongoing referendums about its future.

Key Lessons from Puerto Rico:
* Even after 125+ years, some regions never become full U.S. states.
* Territories can hold multiple referendums on statehood and still not move forward.
* Some regions prefer a hybrid status—neither fully independent nor fully a state.

Biggest Differences from Canada:
- Canada is already independent—it wouldn't start as a U.S. territory like Puerto Rico did.
- Puerto Rico's statehood referendums have been split, while Canada would likely vote decisively one way or another.
- Puerto Rico lacks voting representation in Congress, while Canada would demand full representation immediately.

Would Canada follow Puerto Rico's path?

Maybe... if Canada joined as a special autonomous region instead of a state. This would allow it to keep some independence while benefiting from U.S. economic and security structures.

(In other words: Would Canada want a "best of both worlds" scenario, or would that just be too messy?).

Could Canada Follow a Different Model?

Possible Paths for Canada:

* Texas Model: Become independent first, then voluntarily apply for statehood (unlikely, unless something huge happens).

* Hawaii Model: Gradual integration over decades (only if Canada wanted slow change).

* Puerto Rico Model: Become an autonomous U.S. region without full statehood (most likely if Canada wanted U.S. benefits but some independence).

Or... Canada Could Create a New Model!

- What if Canada joined the U.S. as multiple states, but kept some political autonomy?

- Could Canada become a special "partner state" instead of fully integrating?

- Would the U.S. create a new category of membership just for Canada?

Fun Fact: No U.S. state has ever left the Union (well, except for that little Civil War thing... but we don't talk about that). If Canada joined, it would be a one-way ticket—no turning back!

Final Thoughts: What Can We Learn From History?

Biggest Similarities to Past Cases:

* Like Texas, Canada is an independent nation that could theoretically choose statehood.

* Like Hawaii, Canada has a unique cultural identity that could create resistance.

* Like Puerto Rico, Canada might want a hybrid status instead of full statehood.

Biggest Differences From Past Cases:

* Canada is way bigger and more powerful than any previous statehood case.

* Canada's democratic institutions make it unlikely to be annexed unwillingly.

* Canada's economy and military are already so strong that statehood might not even be necessary.

Would Canada's path to statehood look like Texas, Hawaii, or Puerto Rico?

Or would Canada create a brand-new model of U.S. integration?

| 26 |

Media Narratives

M edia plays a huge role in shaping public perception of political events. If Canada considered joining the U.S., how would different media outlets frame the debate? This chapter explores media bias, propaganda, and the influence of social media on shaping opinions about statehood.

Main Points & Objectives:
- How Would Canadian and U.S. Media Cover the Issue?
- CBC vs. Fox News vs. CNN vs. The New York Times—would their coverage be objective or partisan?
- Would Canadian media resist the idea while U.S. media pushes it?
- Social Media's Role in the Debate
- Twitter (X), TikTok, and Facebook—how would misinformation spread?
- Would Canadian and U.S. politicians use social media campaigns to sway public opinion?
- Could viral trends (like "Make Canada the 51st!") influence real-world decisions?
- Would Media Influence the Referendum Outcome?
- Would news coverage push for fear-mongering ("Loss of sovereignty!") or optimism ("Stronger together!")?

- Would political ads funded by U.S. corporations try to influence Canadian voters?
- Could Foreign Influence Play a Role?
- Would China, Russia, or the EU try to interfere in public discourse?
- Would global propaganda push Canadians away from the U.S.?

Fun Fact: During the 2020 U.S. election, Canadian news stations covered the results as closely as if it were their own election—so imagine the media frenzy if Canada itself were voting on U.S. statehood!

Would the News Help or Hinder Canada's Potential Statehood?

How Would the Media Influence Canada's Decision to Join the U.S.?

If Canada seriously debated becoming a U.S. state, you can bet your last Loonie that the media would go absolutely wild.

Every headline, news segment, and viral TikTok would be either:
Doomsday Scenario: "Canada Losing Its Sovereignty to American Capitalism!"
Patriotic Hype: "Canada and the U.S.: The Ultimate Power Couple!"
Conspiracy Theories: "Is This Just a U.S. Plot to Steal Canada's Maple Syrup Reserves?"

Public opinion wouldn't be shaped just by facts—it would be influenced by spin, media bias, and social media hysteria.

So, how would traditional media, social media, and even foreign propaganda shape the biggest geopolitical debate in modern history?

(Let's just say, this would make Brexit coverage look like a slow news day.)

1. How Would Canadian and U.S. Media Cover the Issue?

Traditional media outlets in both countries would frame the issue very differently.

Canadian Media – The Resistance?

CBC (Canadian Broadcasting Corporation)
- Would likely emphasize Canadian sovereignty and cultural preservation.
- Coverage might include concerns about healthcare, gun laws, and loss of identity.
- Expect a lot of interviews with Quebec politicians saying, "No, merci."

The Globe and Mail & The Toronto Star
- Would likely provide balanced coverage, but still highlight economic concerns and Quebec's objections.
- Editorials would ask, "What would happen to our international reputation?"

National Post & The Western Standard (Alberta-based media)
- Could support statehood, especially in resource-heavy provinces like Alberta (where U.S. energy policies might be more appealing).
- Coverage might argue that Canada would have more influence as U.S. states than as a small, independent country.

Key Media Narratives from Canada:
* "Canada is not for sale."
* "Americans don't even know what poutine is—how can we trust them to govern us?"

* "Could statehood actually be an economic opportunity?"

U.S. Media – The Enthusiasts?

Fox News
- Would likely celebrate statehood as a huge win for U.S. economic and military dominance.
- Could portray opposition as elitist Canadian resistance to common-sense American values.
- Might run segments about how U.S. policies (lower taxes, bigger military, stronger economy) would "help Canada."

CNN & MSNBC
- Would likely cover both sides of the debate, but emphasize concerns over how statehood would affect U.S. politics and democracy.
- Would interview Canadian political experts, some of whom might say, "This is a terrible idea."
- Could focus on cultural tensions ("Would Americans start pronouncing 'Toronto' correctly?").

The New York Times & The Washington Post
- Would analyze the geopolitical and economic consequences of the merger.
- Would publish think pieces like, "Should the U.S. Adopt Canadian Healthcare If This Happens?"

Key Media Narratives from the U.S.:
* "This would be the biggest statehood expansion since the 19th century!"
* "Think of the economic power of a unified North America."
* "Would Canada's progressive politics disrupt U.S. elections?"

(Translation: The media coverage would be all over the place.)

2. Social Media's Role – Would Misinformation Dominate the Debate?

Twitter (X), TikTok, Facebook, and YouTube would explode with hot takes.

Viral Social Media Narratives

Pro-Statehood Hashtags:
* MakeCanadaThe51st
* StrongerTogether
* MapleLeafToStarsAndStripes

Anti-Statehood Hashtags:
* KeepCanadaCanadian
* NoToAnnexation
* EhMeansNo

TikTok Trends:
- Satirical videos: "What if Canadians had to take the U.S. citizenship test?"
- Street interviews in Canada: "Would you rather be American or move to Europe?"
- Misinformation campaigns: "Canada's government is secretly negotiating a deal!" (probably not true).

Twitter/X Arguments in a Nutshell:
- Americans: "This is great! More land, more resources!"
- Canadians: "We don't want your healthcare system or your imperial measurements."
- Europeans: "Wait, Canada isn't already part of the U.S.?"

3. Would Media Coverage Influence the Referendum Outcome?

If a national vote were held, would the media influence the results?

* YES, because...
- Fear-based headlines could make Canadians skeptical.
- U.S. media could paint statehood as an economic no-brainer.
- Political ads funded by corporations could push for integration (think about how much money could be made).

* NO, because...
- Canadians might ignore U.S. media altogether and vote based on local debates.
- Skepticism toward big media outlets is at an all-time high.
- Deep cultural ties to independence could outweigh media influence.

4. Could Foreign Influence Play a Role?

Would China, Russia, or the EU try to interfere in the media debate?

China's Likely View:
* Would oppose statehood—China wants Canada as a neutral trading partner, not an extension of the U.S.
* Could push anti-American propaganda to make Canadians fear annexation.
* Would use state-run media like CGTN and WeChat to promote "Keep Canada independent" narratives.

Russia's Likely View:
* Would see this as U.S. expansionism and a strategic threat to Arctic affairs.
* Might spread misinformation campaigns about U.S. political corruption.

* Would push "Canada is better off with Russia" narratives in on-line forums.

The European Union's View:
- Mixed response—some EU leaders might miss Canada as an independent ally in trade and diplomacy.
- France would be concerned about Quebec—would they push for Quebec's independence?
* Some EU analysts might favor the merger if it meant a stronger NATO and a more stable North American economy.

(Translation: This wouldn't just be a Canadian-American debate—it would be a global media war.)

Final Thoughts: Would Media Coverage Help or Hurt the Debate?

Biggest Media Influences on Public Opinion:
* U.S. media would heavily promote economic and military benefits.
* Canadian media would warn about cultural loss and sovereignty issues.
* Social media would turn the debate into a meme-fueled chaos fest.

Biggest Misinformation Risks:
* Foreign governments could exploit the debate to weaken North American alliances.
* Political ads and social media bots could spread false claims.
* News headlines could distort the issue—turning complex policy into clickbait.

Would Canadians be swayed by U.S. media hype?

Or would they see through the headlines and vote with their gut?

One thing's for sure—this would be the biggest media frenzy in Canadian history.

| 27 |

Sports and Entertainment

Canada's identity is deeply connected to its sports and entertainment industries—from hockey to Canadian film & TV. Would statehood impact its sports leagues, cultural funding, and national pride?

Main Points & Objectives:
- Would Canadian Teams Still Represent Canada in International Sports?
- Would Team Canada still compete in the Olympics, or would Canadian athletes have to compete for the U.S.?
- Would events like the IIHF World Hockey Championship be affected?
- What Happens to the NHL?
- Would teams like the Toronto Maple Leafs and Montreal Canadiens still feel "Canadian"?
- Could the Stanley Cup become a purely American trophy?
- Would more U.S. teams move into Canada due to looser sports market regulations?
- Would Canadian Entertainment Industry Survive?
- Canada funds its own film, music, and TV industry (like CBC and Telefilm Canada)—would these disappear?
- Would Canadian actors, musicians, and filmmakers benefit or suffer from U.S. entertainment dominance?

- Would Canadian sitcoms like Schitt's Creek just become another Hollywood product?

Fun Fact: Without Canada, Hollywood would lose some of its biggest stars! Ryan Reynolds, Keanu Reeves, Jim Carrey, Celine Dion, and Justin Bieber are all Canadian!

Would Canada Lose Its Cultural Identity... or Just Take Over American Sports and Hollywood?

Would Canada's National Pastimes Survive U.S. Statehood?

For many Canadians, sports and entertainment aren't just pastimes—they're a core part of national identity.

- Hockey isn't just a sport—it's practically a religion.
- Canadian musicians, actors, and filmmakers have shaped Hollywood.
- CBC, Canadian film festivals, and cultural funding keep homegrown talent alive.

So, what would happen if Canada became part of the U.S.?
- Would Team Canada disappear from the Olympics?
- Would the NHL become "just another American league"?
- Would Canadian film and TV survive Hollywood's dominance?

Let's break it down—before Don Cherry loses his mind.

1. Would Canadian Teams Still Represent Canada in International Sports?

The Big Question: If Canada became part of the U.S., would Team Canada cease to exist in the Olympics, World Cup, and other international competitions?

Scenario 1: Canada Joins as a U.S. State – No More Team Canada?

- In international tournaments like the Olympics and World Cup, teams represent independent nations—not individual states.

- If Canada fully merged into the U.S., athletes might have to compete under the American flag.

- Say goodbye to gold medal matchups of Team Canada vs. Team USA in hockey—the rivalry would vanish.

(How do we even have an Olympics without that? It would be like peanut butter without jelly.)

Scenario 2: Canada Gets Special Status – "Team Quebec" or "Team Former Canada"?

- Some places, like Puerto Rico and Scotland, have separate Olympic teams despite political ties to a larger country.

- Could Canada negotiate a special exemption to keep its teams?

- Would Quebec push for its own Olympic team—just like it does with everything else?

Fun Fact: The U.K. competes as "Team Great Britain" in the Olympics, but Scotland, Wales, and Northern Ireland compete separately in soccer. Could Canada work out a similar deal?

(If not, expect every Canadian hockey fan to start a petition immediately.)

2. What Happens to the NHL?

Hockey isn't just a sport in Canada—it's a way of life.

So, would the NHL change forever if Canada joined the U.S.?

Would Canadian Teams Still Feel "Canadian"?

- The Toronto Maple Leafs, Montreal Canadiens, and Vancouver Canucks would still exist—but would they feel American?

- Would the Stanley Cup become a purely "U.S. trophy"?

- Would American hockey fans take over "Hockey Night in Canada"? (Perish the thought!).

Could More NHL Teams Move to Canada?

* One upside: If Canada became U.S. states, it might be easier to bring new NHL teams to cities like Quebec City or Hamilton.

* The U.S. sports market is more open to expansion, so maybe Canada would actually get more hockey teams, not fewer.

Fun Fact: The first-ever Stanley Cup was won by a team from Montreal in 1893. If Canada joined the U.S., would that history still belong to Canada... or to America?

(Some traditions should never change, eh?).

3. Would the CFL (Canadian Football League) Survive?

The CFL (Canadian Football League) is one of the last uniquely Canadian sports leagues.

Would It Survive U.S. Statehood?

* Probably not. The CFL would almost certainly be swallowed by the NFL.

* The NFL has never allowed a CFL-U.S. merger—would statehood finally force one?

* Or, could the CFL stay separate as a regional league, like college football?

Fun Fact: The CFL field is bigger than an NFL field (110 yards vs. 100 yards). Would American teams have to learn the Canadian version of football if they merged?

(Would Americans ever allow "three downs instead of four"? Probably not.)

4. Would Canada's Entertainment Industry Survive?

Canada's film, TV, and music industries have built a strong identity—so would statehood mean the end of uniquely Canadian entertainment?

Would Hollywood Dominate Canadian Media?
- Canada has strict media protection laws that require a percentage of TV and radio to be "Canadian content."
- If Canada became part of the U.S., those laws might disappear—letting Hollywood take over.
- Would CBC, Canada's national broadcaster, survive... or be absorbed by American networks?

(Would we still get classic Canadian comedies like "Schitt's Creek," or would everything just be reruns of "Friends"?)

What About Canadian Music & Film?
- Many of the biggest stars in music and film are Canadian—Ryan Reynolds, Celine Dion, Drake, Justin Bieber, etc.
- Would Canadian artists still get special funding and grants?
- Or would they have to compete in the massive U.S. market with no support?

Fun Fact: "Titanic" was directed by a Canadian (James Cameron), and most of it was filmed in Canada. Would it now count as an "American" movie?

(Someone call Leonardo DiCaprio—this is serious!).

5. Would Canadian Culture Disappear... or Take Over the U.S.?

Some Fear: The "Americanization" of Canada
- Would Canadian accents, slang, and traditions fade away?
- Would Tim Hortons become just another Starbucks subsidiary?
- Would Canadian Thanksgiving be moved to November, just like in the U.S.? (The horror!).

The Alternative: Canada Takes Over American Culture!
- What if, instead of Canada losing its identity, it reshaped American pop culture?
- Would hockey become as popular as the NFL?
- Would more Canadian actors, musicians, and directors dominate Hollywood?

Fun Fact: If Canada became a U.S. state, "Hockey Night in Canada" could be broadcast across the entire U.S.! (Look out, baseball—you're in trouble!).

Final Thoughts: Would Sports & Entertainment Survive?

Biggest Wins for Canada:
* More funding and exposure for sports teams and entertainment industries.
* Easier access to U.S. media and sports markets.
* Could actually grow Canada's influence in global pop culture.

Biggest Risks for Canada:
* Might lose control over cultural policies and funding.
* Could see uniquely Canadian leagues (like CFL) disappear.
* Would Canada's sports and entertainment still feel "Canadian"... or just become part of the U.S.?

Would Canada's unique identity survive U.S. statehood?

Or would hockey, film, and music just become "another part of America"?

One thing's for sure—the Stanley Cup better never, EVER be renamed.

(Because if that happens, Canadians WILL riot.)

| 28 |

Tourism and Infrastructure

Canada and the U.S. have one of the largest shared tourism markets in the world. But if Canada became part of the U.S., what would happen to borders, travel, tourism, and infrastructure?

Main Points & Objectives:
- Would the U.S.-Canada Border Disappear?
- No more passports needed between the two nations?
- Would new states have "state lines" instead of international borders?
- Impact on Tourism Industry
- Would Canada lose tourism dollars if it's no longer seen as an "international destination"?
- Would U.S. tourism chains take over Canadian travel hotspots?
- Would Niagara Falls be just another American tourist trap instead of an international landmark?
- Changes in Transportation & Infrastructure
- Would major Canadian airlines (Air Canada, WestJet) merge with U.S. carriers?
- Would train travel improve with U.S. Amtrak integration?
- Would Canada's strict environmental policies on transportation be loosened under U.S. jurisdiction?

Fun Fact: The U.S.-Canada border is the longest international border in the world—over 5,500 miles long! If Canada became part of the U.S., the U.S. would technically have no northern border!

Would Traveling in North America Get Easier... or Just Weirder?

Would Canada Still Feel Like a Foreign Destination?

Right now, Canada and the U.S. have one of the largest shared tourism markets in the world.

- Millions of Americans visit Canada every year for its beautiful landscapes, ski resorts, and poutine (and to escape Florida's heat in the summer).
- Millions of Canadians visit the U.S. to go to Disney World, shop at Target, and escape winter (except for those who actually enjoy -40°C, which is just suspicious behavior).

But if Canada became part of the U.S., how would travel, tourism, and transportation change?
- Would there still be a "border" or just a state line?
- Would Canadian airlines merge into U.S. carriers?
- Would Niagara Falls just become another American roadside attraction with overpriced souvenirs?

Let's dive into the potential travel transformations—and see if this makes vacations better or just messier.

1. Would the U.S.-Canada Border Disappear?

The Big Question: If Canada became part of the U.S., would travelers still need passports to go between former Canada and the U.S.?

Scenario 1: No More International Border – Just State Lines

* If Canada were fully absorbed into the U.S., the current international border would disappear.

* Traveling between Toronto and New York would be like driving from Ohio to Pennsylvania—no passports, no customs.

* Airports wouldn't need international terminals for U.S.-Canada flights anymore.

(Imagine never having to deal with border security between the U.S. and Canada again—just a guy in a neon vest waving you through a toll road.)

Scenario 2: Some Border Restrictions Remain

- The U.S. might still keep a form of border control for security reasons (TSA never misses an opportunity to ask people to take off their shoes).

- If Canada joined as multiple states instead of one, could some regions negotiate different rules on travel?

- Quebec might demand a special status, requiring French-language customs officers (who would glare at Americans who don't know what "bonjour" means).

Fun Fact: Right now, the U.S.-Canada border is the longest undefended border in the world—over 5,500 miles long. If Canada became part of the U.S., America would technically have no northern border at all! (Alaska would suddenly feel very lonely up there).

2. Impact on the Tourism Industry – Would Canada Lose Its Appeal?

Right now, Canada is an international travel destination. People visit to experience:

- Vancouver's mountains and beaches
- The Northern Lights in the Yukon
- French culture in Quebec

- Banff and Jasper's jaw-dropping landscapes
- Poutine, maple syrup, and Tim Hortons coffee

But if Canada became a U.S. state... would it still feel "special" to tourists?

Would U.S. Tourists Still Visit If Canada Isn't "Foreign"?
- Some Americans love visiting Canada because it's an "international" experience without needing to fly overseas.
- If Canada became just another part of the U.S., would it lose the "exotic" factor that draws visitors?
- Would places like Quebec City lose tourism because Americans could just visit New Orleans for a similar French-influenced experience?

(Would visiting Toronto still feel different from visiting Chicago? Or would it all just blend together?)

Would U.S. Businesses Take Over Canadian Tourism?
- Would McDonald's, Starbucks, and Walmart flood even the most remote Canadian travel spots?
- Could U.S. hotel chains dominate areas that were previously home to unique, local tourism businesses?
- Would Niagara Falls turn into a massive, overpriced, over-commercialized American tourist trap (think Las Vegas but with more mist and fewer Elvis impersonators)?

Fun Fact: Right now, the Canadian side of Niagara Falls is considered "the better side" with the best views. Would Americans finally win the Great Niagara Debate if it all became U.S. land?

3. Changes in Transportation & Infrastructure

Would merging the U.S. and Canada actually make travel more efficient?

Would Canadian Airlines Merge with U.S. Carriers?
- Air Canada and WestJet are major international airlines—would they merge with U.S. airlines like American Airlines or Delta?
- Would Canadian airports become U.S. hubs instead of independent travel centers?
- Would flight prices drop or rise with U.S. airline competition?

(Would budget airlines like Spirit Airlines finally start flying to Canada? Would anyone actually want that?)

Would Train Travel Improve?
- Right now, Canada's VIA Rail system is separate from Amtrak—would they finally merge into one system?
- Could high-speed rail finally be built between Canadian and U.S. cities (hello, Toronto to New York in 3 hours!).
- Would long-distance train travel become easier or just as painfully slow as Amtrak currently is?

Fun Fact: The Trans-Canada Highway is one of the longest roads in the world. Would it still be called the Trans-Canada Highway... or would the U.S. rename it? ("The Maple Route" sounds pretty catchy though...).

4. Would U.S. Travel Laws Take Over?

If Canada became a U.S. state, it would have to follow U.S. travel regulations.

- Would TSA rules apply at Canadian airports? (Translation: More security screenings, more shoe removal, and no large maple syrup bottles in carry-on bags).

- Would U.S. travel restrictions apply? (Example: If the U.S. bans travel to a country, would Canadian travelers also be affected?).

- Would Canada's strong environmental protections on airlines and transportation be relaxed?

(Would Canadians finally have to embrace "Real ID" laws, or would they just keep showing their hockey season tickets as identification?)

Final Thoughts: Would Travel Be Better or Worse?

Biggest Wins for Canada:
* Easier border crossings—no more passports or customs.
* Potential improvements to air and rail travel.
* Better tourism promotion as part of a unified U.S. travel market.

Biggest Risks for Canada:
* Might lose its appeal as an "international" destination.
* Could see an influx of big U.S. chains taking over local tourism businesses.
* Would have to follow stricter U.S. travel laws.

Would Canadians enjoy a border-free North America?

Or would they miss the feeling of being a separate, unique destination?

One thing's for sure—if the Canadian side of Niagara Falls ever turns into a Vegas-style theme park, expect a national crisis.

| 29 |

Future Scenarios

I f Canada joined the U.S., what would the world look like in 50 years? Would it be a thriving superstate, or would the merger cause unexpected problems? This chapter presents various possible futures based on political, economic, and social trends.

Main Points & Objectives:
- Scenario 1: A Prosperous North American Superpower
- Canada's natural resources + U.S. economy = unprecedented global dominance.
- Unified trade, infrastructure, and military create the strongest geopolitical force in history.
- Former Canadians feel culturally integrated but still proud of their regional identity.
- Scenario 2: A Political Disaster Leading to Secession
- Political and cultural divides deepen, leading to calls for Quebec, Alberta, or BC to secede.
- U.S. partisanship infects Canada's historically moderate politics, creating unrest.
- Canada's healthcare system collapses under U.S. privatization pressure.
- Scenario 3: A Hybrid System (Not Fully U.S., Not Fully Canada)
- Canada retains autonomous governance but benefits from U.S. resources.

- A "Canada Special Status" is created, like Puerto Rico but with more autonomy.

- U.S. and Canadian cultures mix, but key differences (healthcare, education, language laws) remain.

- Scenario 4: Canada Never Joins the U.S., But Becomes More Integrated

- Even if full statehood never happens, Canada and the U.S. merge economies and defense even further.

- The border becomes virtually invisible, and policies align without losing sovereignty.

Fun Fact: If Canada and the U.S. fully merged, their combined GDP would be over $30 trillion—far ahead of China and the EU!

Would Canada Become a Superpower... or Regret Everything?

What Would North America Look Like in 50 Years If Canada Became a U.S. State?

Let's fast forward half a century. The year is 2075. Self-driving cars are everywhere (except in Montreal, where people still drive like maniacs). The U.S. has had at least three reality-TV-star Presidents. The NHL has expanded to Mars.

And Canada? Well... that depends.

Would the U.S.-Canada merger be a global success story or a total disaster? Would Canadians still feel Canadian, or would they be fully Americanized (but still saying "sorry" too much)?

Let's explore four possible future scenarios, from best-case utopia to worst-case chaos.

Scenario 1: A Prosperous North American Superpower

Outcome: Canada and the U.S. thrive together, forming the most powerful economic, political, and military alliance in history.

Key Features of This Future:
* The U.S.-Canada economy dominates the world—with a combined GDP over $30 trillion (larger than China and the EU combined!).
* Natural resources + tech innovation = unmatched global influence (Alberta's oil + Silicon Valley = economic gold).
* Trade and transportation boom—high-speed rail from Vancouver to Miami becomes a reality (goodbye, long TSA lines!).
* Canada retains cultural identity but embraces U.S. opportunities—hockey is still king, but so is the NFL.
* The unified North American military is unstoppable—the Arctic is fully secured, and global alliances are stronger than ever.

Biggest Winners in This Scenario:
- Businesses and workers—free movement and investment create endless jobs.
- Canada's energy sector—with U.S. backing, it dominates the global market.
- Tourism—no borders mean Americans visit Banff like they visit Yellowstone.

(This is the future where America finally learns to love Tim Hortons and poutine.)

Scenario 2: A Political Disaster Leading to Secession

Outcome: Instead of unifying, Canada fractures into political chaos, leading to new secession movements and internal conflict.

Key Features of This Future:

* Cultural tensions explode—Quebec, Alberta, and British Columbia threaten to secede.

* U.S. partisanship infects Canada's politics, splitting regions between far-right and far-left factions.

* Canadian healthcare collapses under U.S. privatization—Canadians are furious when a simple doctor visit suddenly costs $500.

* Mass protests break out—Canada's famous politeness disappears as citizens demand independence from Washington, D.C.

* In 2080, a new referendum is held—Quebec officially leaves, Alberta threatens civil war, and Vancouver just wants to be left alone.

Biggest Losers in This Scenario:

- The average Canadian—loses healthcare benefits, pays higher taxes, and gets stuck in a divided political mess.

- The U.S. government—suddenly dealing with Canadian separatist movements (because one Civil War wasn't enough?).

- Businesses—uncertainty kills investment, and economic collapse follows.

(This is the future where Canadians say, "We made a huge mistake, eh.")

Scenario 3: A Hybrid System – Not Fully U.S., Not Fully Canada

Outcome: Canada joins the U.S. in some ways but keeps its independence in others—creating a unique, semi-autonomous status.

Key Features of This Future:

Canada technically becomes U.S. states, but with a special status (like Puerto Rico, but with more maple syrup).

The Canadian healthcare system survives—but only in former Canadian states.

Quebec keeps its own legal and language protections, making it the most independent U.S. state ever.

Canada's military is integrated into the U.S., but with separate units (kind of like how the UK operates within NATO).

Major Canadian traditions remain intact—Hockey Night in Canada still exists, and Thanksgiving stays in October.

Biggest Trade-Offs in This Scenario:

- Pros: Canada keeps its social programs but benefits from U.S. economic strength.

- Cons: Unclear identity—not fully American, but not fully independent.

(This is the future where Canadians say, "Okay, we're kind of American, but not really, okay?")

Scenario 4: Canada Never Joins the U.S., But Becomes More Integrated

Outcome: Canada never officially becomes a U.S. state, but the two nations become so integrated that borders barely matter anymore.

Key Features of This Future:

The U.S. and Canada form a stronger North American economic and defense alliance, similar to the European Union.

Borders become nearly invisible—citizens can live and work freely between the two countries.

The military becomes more unified—Canada and the U.S. share Arctic defense and strategic planning.

Canadian businesses operate under U.S. regulations but still keep national identity (Tim Hortons remains proudly Canadian).

Major policy alignment happens—tax laws, environmental policies, and infrastructure projects sync up.

Biggest Winners in This Scenario:

- Trade and business—companies move seamlessly between both markets.

- Tourists and travelers—moving between Canada and the U.S. becomes as easy as crossing state lines.

- Both governments—they get the benefits of integration without full political headaches.

(This is the future where Americans say, "Wait, Canada wasn't already part of the U.S.?")

Final Thoughts: Which Future Is Most Likely?

Most Optimistic Scenario:
- Scenario 1 (Superpower Union)—if both nations truly commit to working together.

Most Chaotic Scenario:
- Scenario 2 (Political Disaster & Secession)—if cultural tensions explode.

Most Realistic Scenario?
- Scenario 4 (Deeper Integration Without Statehood)—because the U.S. and Canada already work together so closely, this is the most logical outcome.

Would Canada fully become part of the U.S. in the next 50 years?

Or would it just become an unofficial partner—economically, politically, and militarily—while keeping its independence?

One thing's for sure: No matter what happens, Canadians will still insist their version of ketchup chips is superior.

| 30 |

Conclusion: Thought Experiment or Future Reality?

S ummarizing everything—is this idea crazy or feasible?

Key Topics:
- Could Canada ever actually vote for this?
- What would it take politically, legally, and economically?
- What does this thought experiment reveal about U.S.-Canada relations?

Final Thought: Whether or not it ever happens, exploring this scenario teaches us about national identity, geopolitics, and the evolving nature of global alliances.

This book delivers a fascinating, thought-provoking, and entertaining look at a hypothetical but serious discussion: What if Canada joined the United States?

With humor, fun facts, political analysis, and historical deep dives, this book offers something for everyone—from history buffs to political junkies, and even those who just love a good dad joke.

Was This Just a Fun Political Exercise... or Could It Actually Happen?

So... Could Canada Ever Actually Join the U.S.?

After 30 chapters, thousands of dad jokes, and enough political analysis to impress even the nerdiest of historians, we're left with one big question:

Is Canada joining the U.S. a ridiculous fantasy... or a legitimate possibility?

Well, let's break it down one last time.

1. Could Canada Ever Actually Vote for This?

Would Canadians ever vote to join the U.S.?
- In polls and surveys, the idea of merging with the U.S. has never gained serious traction—even in the most politically aligned regions.
- Quebec would likely oppose it outright, and many provinces would resist losing their national identity.
- The Canadian political system is designed for sovereignty—shifting to a U.S. model would be a legal and logistical nightmare.

The Verdict?
It would take an enormous political and cultural shift for Canada to even consider voting on this. Right now, it's not even close to reality.

(Translation: Don't hold your breath, America.)

2. What Would It Take Politically, Legally, and Economically?

Even if Canadians somehow changed their minds, this wouldn't happen overnight.

Political Hurdles:
- A national referendum would be required in Canada, and possibly individual provincial votes.
- The U.S. Congress would have to approve it, which could take years.
- Would Canada join as one state or multiple? (Cue endless political debates in Washington.)

Economic Adjustments:
- Would Canada adopt the U.S. dollar?
- Would taxes increase or decrease?
- Would Canadian businesses benefit, or would they be swallowed by U.S. corporations?

Legal Chaos:
- Would Canadian laws be rewritten to match U.S. laws?
- Would healthcare remain universal, or would provinces fight to keep their systems?
- Would Quebec demand a special political status? (Spoiler alert: Absolutely.)

The Verdict?
Even if everyone agreed, this process would take at least 10-20 years, if not longer. (Think Brexit, but more polite and with more maple syrup references.)

(Translation: By the time this actually happened, we'd probably have flying cars.)

3. What Does This Thought Experiment Reveal About U.S.-Canada Relations?

Even if this scenario is unlikely, this book has taught us a lot about how closely Canada and the U.S. are already connected.

Canada and the U.S. already share:
* A massive trade relationship (USMCA, formerly NAFTA)
* A strong military alliance (NATO & NORAD)
* Deep cultural ties (Hollywood, music, sports)
* Millions of dual-citizenship families and cross-border workers

- So, if Canada and the U.S. are already so close, why isn't this even a debate?
- National identity still matters. Canadians take pride in their unique history, culture, and government.
- Some policies are simply too different. Healthcare, gun laws, and government structure are major sticking points.
- Political partisanship in the U.S. makes this idea even less appealing to Canadians who prefer a more moderate system.

The Verdict?
Canada and the U.S. are likely to remain separate—but they may continue to integrate economically and politically in new ways.

(Translation: We'll be best friends, but probably never roommates.)

Final Verdict: Will This Ever Happen?

Most Likely Outcome?
* No, Canada will not become part of the U.S. in our lifetime. The cultural, political, and legal hurdles are simply too big.

What Could Happen Instead?

* Canada and the U.S. may continue integrating policies, trade, and defense agreements.

* Border restrictions may ease further, allowing for even freer movement.

* Some regions (like Alberta) may push for closer ties to the U.S. in economic policy.

Biggest Takeaway?

Even if this is a fun political what-if, it highlights how closely linked Canada and the U.S. already are.

(Translation: We're already a dysfunctional family, we just don't live under the same roof.)

Why This Book Matters

This book wasn't just about whether Canada should become a U.S. state—it was about exploring national identity, geopolitics, and the future of alliances in an increasingly connected world.

* It made us think about how borders shape our perceptions of nationhood.

* It highlighted the strengths and weaknesses of both systems.

* It reminded us that politics and history are filled with weird, surprising possibilities.

And, of course...

* It gave us plenty of dad jokes, hockey references, and maple syrup metaphors.

Whether or not Canada ever becomes a U.S. state, one thing is certain:

America will always love Canadian bacon, and Canada will always love judging America's healthcare system.

And that's what true friendship is all about.

The End – Or Just the Beginning of More Fun Geopolitical Debates?

APPENDICES

Additional Resources, Fun Extras, and
Extra Canadian Goodness

Appendix A: Quick Reference – Key Facts & Figures

U.S. & Canada at a Glance

Category	Canada	United States
Population	~39 million	~332 million
Land Area	9.98 million km² (2nd largest in world)	9.83 million km² (3rd largest in world)
GDP (Nominal)	~$2.1 trillion	~$26 trillion
Official Languages	English, French	English (Spanish widely spoken)
Healthcare	Universal healthcare (public)	Mixed public/private system
Gun Laws	Strict regulations	Varies by state (2nd Amendment)
Drinking Age	18-19 (varies by province)	21 nationwide
Thanksgiving	2nd Monday in October	4th Thursday in November
Biggest Trading Partner	United States	Canada

Appendix B: Timeline of Key U.S.-Canada Relations Events

Historic Moments in U.S.-Canada Relations

1776 – American Revolution begins; some Canadians support the British, others join the revolution.

1812 – War of 1812: U.S. tries (and fails) to invade Canada. Canada burns down the White House in return (oops!).

1867 – Canada officially becomes a country with Confederation (but still remains under British rule).

1931 – Canada gains full legislative independence from Britain (but still keeps the Queen).

1949 – Canada joins NATO as a founding member, solidifying its alliance with the U.S.

1965 – Canada gets its own flag (no more borrowing Britain's!).

1988 – U.S.-Canada Free Trade Agreement (FTA) is signed, later expanded into NAFTA (1994).

2001 – 9/11 leads to tighter border security between the U.S. and Canada.

2020 – COVID-19 pandemic temporarily closes the U.S.-Canada border (first time since 1812!).

(Fun Fact: The longest undefended border in the world? The U.S.-Canada border, at over 5,500 miles!)

Appendix C: Potential U.S. State Names for Canadian Provinces

If Canada joined the U.S. as multiple states, what might they be called?

Current Canadian Provinces → Potential U.S. States

Canadian Province/Territory	Potential U.S. State Name
British Columbia	"Cascadia" or "Pacific Columbia"
Alberta	"North Texas" or "Big Sky State"
Saskatchewan	"Great Plains State"
Manitoba	"Midwest North"
Ontario	"Lakeshore State"
Quebec	"French America" (if they agree!)
Newfoundland & Labrador	"Atlantic State"
Nova Scotia	"New Scotland" (already means that!)
New Brunswick	"Acadia"
Prince Edward Island	"Smallest State" (Sorry, Rhode Island!)
Yukon	"Arctic Alaska"
Northwest Territories	"Northern Lights State"
Nunavut	"Inuit State" (First Indigenous-majority state?)

(Would Quebec even join, or would it pull a Texas and stay independent first?)

Appendix D: Common Canadian vs. American Phrases – Would Language Change?

Canadian Sayings vs. American Sayings

Canadian Phrase	American Equivalent
-	
"Toque" (warm hat)	"Beanie"
"Eh?" (friendly tag question)	"Huh?" or "Right?"
"Loonie" / "Toonie" (coins)	Just... "one dollar" / "two dollars"
"Poutine" (fries, gravy, cheese curds)	"Fries with stuff on top"
"Washroom"	"Restroom" or "Bathroom"
"Runners" (sneakers)	"Tennis shoes"
"Pop" (soft drink)	"Soda"

(Would the U.S. adopt "washroom," or would Canadians be forced to say "restroom"? The horror!)

Appendix E: Best Canadian Contributions to the U.S.

Did you know some of the biggest things in American culture actually came from Canada?

Famous Canadian Inventions:
* Basketball (invented by Canadian James Naismith)
* Hawaiian Pizza (invented in Ontario – pineapple haters, blame Canada!)
* IMAX Theaters (invented in Canada – your 3D movie nausea is their fault!)
* Insulin (a Canadian discovery that changed medicine forever!)
* Trivial Pursuit (the game that makes family game night way too competitive!)

Famous Canadian Actors in Hollywood:
* Ryan Reynolds
* Keanu Reeves
* Jim Carrey
* Rachel McAdams
* Seth Rogen
* Sandra Oh

Famous Canadian Musicians Who Took Over the U.S.:
* Celine Dion
* Drake
* The Weeknd
* Justin Bieber (sorry!)
* Shania Twain (let's go, girls!)

* Alanis Morissette

(Would the U.S. get automatic bragging rights over these Canadians if Canada joined?)

Appendix F: Further Reading & Resources

Want to dive even deeper into U.S.-Canada relations, statehood history, and geopolitical debates? Here are some great books, articles, and documentaries to check out:

- Books & Reports:
- Merger of the Century – Diane Francis (Exploring Canada-U.S. economic integration)
- Destiny of the Republic – Candice Millard (A historical look at U.S. state expansions)
- Borders and Bridges: Canada-U.S. Relations in the 21st Century – Multiple Authors

  Documentaries & Films:
- The War of 1812 (PBS) – How Canada and the U.S. fought over borders.
- Inside Canada's Parliament (CBC) – A deep dive into Canadian governance.
- The Corporation (2003) – A Canadian documentary about business influence on politics.

  Online Resources:
- U.S. Congressional Research Service (CRS) Reports on U.S.-Canada trade.
- Government of Canada's official reports on U.S.-Canada relations.

- The Wilson Center's Canada Institute (U.S.-Canada policy research).

(Because let's be real, this topic is fun but also a real geopolitical discussion!)

U.S. CONGRESSIONAL BILL DRAFT

Here's a draft of a U.S. Statehood Bill detailing the process by which Canada would be incorporated into the United States. It includes provisions for legal, economic, and political integration while outlining the necessary steps for a smooth transition.

U.S. CONGRESSIONAL BILL (DRAFT)
The Canada Statehood and Integration Act of [Year]

A BILL

To provide for the admission of the nation of Canada, including its provinces and territories, as one or more states of the United States of America, and for other purposes related to the political, economic, and legal integration of Canada into the Union.

SECTION 1. SHORT TITLE

This Act may be cited as the "Canada Statehood and Integration Act."

SECTION 2. FINDINGS

Congress finds that—

1. The United States and Canada share the longest undefended border in the world and maintain strong economic, military, and diplomatic ties;

2. Canada has expressed interest in closer integration with the United States, including the potential for statehood, through a national referendum approved by the Canadian people;

3. The integration of Canada as U.S. states will enhance North American economic security, strengthen defense cooperation, and promote democratic values;

4. The legal and constitutional frameworks for Canadian provinces and territories must be aligned with U.S. law to facilitate a smooth transition;

5. The people of Canada shall be granted full rights and privileges as U.S. citizens, including representation in Congress and participation in federal elections.

SECTION 3. PROCEDURE FOR STATEHOOD APPLICATION AND ADMISSION

(a) Formal Petition by Canada

- The Canadian Parliament shall submit a formal request for U.S. statehood upon a majority vote (50%+1) in a national referendum.

- Each province and territory shall conduct its own referendum to determine whether it will join the U.S. as a separate state, as part of a larger state, or remain outside U.S. jurisdiction.

(b) Congressional Approval

- Upon receipt of Canada's request, the United States Congress shall conduct hearings to review the application.

- Admission shall require a majority vote in the House of Representatives and Senate, and presidential approval.

(c) State Designation and Representation

- Canada's provinces and territories may enter the U.S. as individual states or as a unified state.
- Each new state shall be entitled to congressional representation based on its population.
- Each new state shall receive two Senators and appropriate House Representatives per Article I, Section 2 of the U.S. Constitution.

(d) Transition Government

- Upon admission, Canada shall be placed under a Transition Commission for up to five years, during which Canadian legal and political systems will be aligned with U.S. federal and state structures.

SECTION 4. LEGAL INTEGRATION

(a) Constitutional Compliance

- Canadian laws and provincial constitutions shall be reviewed for compliance with the U.S. Constitution, Bill of Rights, and federal law.
- The Canadian Charter of Rights and Freedoms may be incorporated into state constitutions where applicable.

(b) Legal System Transition

- Canadian courts shall transition into the U.S. judicial system, with provincial supreme courts becoming state supreme courts.
- Canadian legal standards (e.g., criminal law, healthcare laws) shall be gradually harmonized with U.S. laws over a ten-year period.

(c) Quebec Special Status

- Quebec shall be granted linguistic and legal autonomy, allowing the province to retain French as an official state language and elements of its civil law system.

SECTION 5. ECONOMIC AND MONETARY INTEGRATION

(a) Adoption of the U.S. Dollar
- The United States Dollar (USD) shall become the official currency of all newly admitted states.
- A five-year transition period shall be provided for currency conversion.

(b) Trade and Economic Transition
- All trade agreements currently held by Canada shall be renegotiated under U.S. jurisdiction.
- Canadian industries shall be granted a ten-year economic adjustment period for compliance with U.S. labor laws, taxation, and federal regulations.

(c) Banking and Financial System Alignment
- Canadian banks shall transition to comply with U.S. banking regulations and be eligible for Federal Deposit Insurance Corporation (FDIC) protection.

SECTION 6. SOCIAL AND CULTURAL POLICIES

(a) Healthcare and Social Services
- Canada's universal healthcare system may be preserved as a state-administered program with federal funding considerations.

- Social Security, Medicare, and Medicaid shall be extended to Canadian residents upon statehood recognition.

(b) Education and Language Rights
- Canadian educational institutions shall transition to U.S. Department of Education standards.
- French language protections shall be upheld in Quebec and bilingual regions.

SECTION 7. MILITARY AND BORDER TRANSITION

(a) U.S. Military Integration
- The Canadian Armed Forces shall be merged with the United States Armed Forces, with options for personnel to retain rank and position.
- Existing Canadian military bases shall be incorporated into the U.S. Department of Defense structure.

(b) Border and Immigration Adjustments
- The U.S.-Canada border shall be dissolved, and former border control facilities shall be repurposed.
- Canadian passport holders shall be automatically granted U.S. citizenship upon statehood ratification.
- All immigration policies between the two nations shall be fully unified.

SECTION 8. IMPLEMENTATION TIMELINE

The following timeline shall be established for Canada's integration:

Year 1-2 – National referendum in Canada, Congressional hearings in the U.S.

Year 3-5 – Legal and constitutional alignment begins. U.S. Dollar introduced in Canada.

Year 6-10 – Full political, military, and economic integration completed. First Canadian Senators and Representatives elected to U.S. Congress.

SECTION 9. FINAL PROVISIONS

(a) Sovereignty Clause
- Canada's provinces shall retain state-level governance but will be fully subject to the U.S. Constitution and federal law.

(b) Repeal of Previous Treaties
- All prior treaties between the U.S. and Canada that conflict with this Act shall be nullified upon ratification.

(c) Enactment
- This Act shall take effect immediately upon passage and signature by the President of the United States.

Final Thought from the Author

Whether you picked up this book for a serious geopolitical analysis, a fun thought experiment, or just to laugh at some Canada-U.S. jokes, I hope you've enjoyed the ride.

This topic isn't just about politics—it's about what makes a country unique, what binds nations together, and how the world's biggest partnerships evolve over time.

(Now, let's all grab a double-double and celebrate our shared love of over-apologizing and complaining about the weather!)

Cheers to the U.S. & Canada—neighbors, friends, and the ultimate sibling rivalry!

About the Author

JD Rossetti is a seasoned public affairs professional, which is a fancy way of saying he's spent over a decade navigating the world of government relations, legislative affairs, public administration, and policy analysis—without losing his sense of humor (or his hair... mostly). With a knack for advocacy, strategic planning, and community engagement, JD has dedicated his career to shaping public policy and making a real difference.

A former Washington State Representative, JD tackled big issues like education, infrastructure, economic development, and public health—because someone had to. He successfully secured funding for education, mental health initiatives, and broadband expansion, ensuring that students could learn, communities could thrive, and people could finally stream their favorite shows without buffering. As a School Board Director, he championed student success, technology integration, and budget oversight, proving that yes, numbers can be fun (sometimes).

JD holds a Master of Public Administration (MPA) from The Evergreen State College and a Bachelor of Arts in Public Affairs from Washington State University. Passionate about public service, policy innovation, and effective governance, JD continues to work toward policies that strengthen and support communities—one well-crafted policy (and dad joke) at a time.

jdrossetti.com